Learning or.

In this much-needed book, you'll learn how incorporating physical activity into the classroom can improve students' engagement, achievement, and overall wellness. Students typically spend most of the day sitting at their desks, and many don't have recess or PE, yet research shows that regular exercise helps stimulate brain function and improve skills such as reading, critical thinking, organization, and focus. Authors Brad Johnson and Melody Jones, who have consulted with schools across the globe on fitness issues, offer a variety of games and activities you can use to integrate exercise into any class or subject area. You'll learn how to:

- Create an "active classroom" with active workstations and fitness areas to keep students alert and engaged throughout the day;
- Gradually introduce physical activities into your everyday classroom routine;
- Use interactive technology to teach your students about health and fitness;
- Try out a variety of activities and exercises to reduce stress, help students focus, promote teamwork, build core strength and balance, and more;
- Make STEM classes more exciting with hands-on activities, projects, and real-world problems, all while getting your students up and moving.

These activities are easy to implement and are designed to improve one's physical and mental capabilities, as well as increase enjoyment of learning for happier, healthier, higher-achieving students.

Brad Johnson is an international speaker in the field of education. He recently spent time in Malaysia developing a fitness diploma with their Ministry of Education.

Melody Jones is certified through the National Academy of Sports Medicine as a Youth Exercise Specialist, Fitness Nutrition Specialist, and Weight Loss Specialist.

Learning on Your Feet

Incorporating Physical Activity into the K-8 Classroom

Brad Johnson and Melody Jones

Routledge
Taylor & Francis Group
NEW YORK AND LONDON

First published 2016
by Routledge
711 Third Avenue, New York, NY 10017

and by Routledge
2 Park Square, Milton Park, Abingdon, Oxon, OX14 4RN

Routledge is an imprint of the Taylor & Francis Group, an informa business

Library of Congress Cataloging in Publication Data

Names: Johnson, Brad, 1969- | Jones, Melody.
Title: Learning on your feet : incorporating physical activity into the K-8 classroom / by Brad Johnson and Melody Jones.
Description: New York : Routledge, 2016. | Includes bibliographical references.
Identifiers: LCCN 2015042666| ISBN 9781138956773 (hardback) | ISBN 9781138956780 (pbk.) | ISBN 9781315665559 (ebook)
Subjects: LCSH: Movement education. | Learning—Physiological aspects.
Classification: LCC GV452 .J635 2016 | DDC 372.86—dc23
LC record available at http://lccn.loc.gov/2015042666

ISBN: 978-1-138-95677-3 (hbk)
ISBN: 978-1-138-95678-0 (pbk)
ISBN: 978-1-315-66555-9 (ebk)

Typeset in Optima
by Cenveo Publisher Services

Contents

Contents

Meet the Authors

Dr. Brad Johnson is an international speaker in the field of education. He is author of *What Schools Don't Teach: 20 Ways to Help Students Excel in School and Life* (Routledge), as well as *From School Administrator to School Leader: 15 Keys to Maximizing Your Leadership Potential* (Routledge). Dr. Johnson has over 20 years' experience at the K-12 and collegiate level.

Dr. Johnson is a former athlete and competitive bodybuilder. He has also coached athletes at the high school and collegiate level. He recently spent time in Malaysia developing a fitness diploma with their Ministry of Education. He trained teachers throughout Malaysia to incorporate more fitness into the classroom.

Melody Jones is one of the top functional training experts in the country. She is certified through The National Academy of Sports Medicine. She is also certified through NASM as a Youth Exercise Specialist, Fitness Nutrition Specialist, and Weight Loss Specialist. In her practice, she focuses on rehabilitation and injury prevention training with special and general populations. Ms. Jones

also works with schools on developing activities to improve balance, coordination, and core for the classroom, physical education, and after school programs.

For more information or to inquire about speaking or workshops, please contact us at www.Learningonyourfeet.com

Preface

"Physical fitness is not only one of the most important keys to a healthy body; it is the basis of dynamic and creative intellectual activity."

John F. Kennedy

Some of my (Brad) favorite childhood memories involve the playground and recess during elementary school. I remember going to recess in the morning and when we finished lunch we could go out for recess. Needless to say it didn't take me long to finish lunch and race out to my favorite spot in school, the playground! I was a straight "A" student, but I also had a lot of energy and so I needed recess and physical education to burn off the excess energy. I remember once in 2nd grade, I was actually skipping down the hall on our way back from the library when my teacher saw me; she pulled me to the side and spanked me in the hallway. Many children today may not even know how to skip, and I was getting beat for it in school! I can't even imagine the trouble and spankings I would have gotten if I hadn't have had recess and other opportunities to burn off energy. Honestly, I would have rather gotten the spanking than to have missed PE or recess. And while she did spank me that once, I'm sure I still skipped down the hall many times when she wasn't looking. Compared to how we educate children today, I was fortunate to attend school during a time when recess, play, and physical activity were an integral part of the learning experience and where we had opportunities to learn like children do, actively!

Unfortunately, most students today don't have the opportunity to move, explore, play, and burn off their excess energy. Instead, we think school is supposed to be all about sitting at a desk and studying to pass a test. As early as the 1980s and 1990s, recess and physical activity was becoming a target of public education. "We are intent on improving academic performance," said Benjamin O. Canada, then superintendent of schools in Atlanta. "You don't do that by having kids hanging on the monkey bars." However, as the research throughout this book will overwhelmingly show, this misguided thinking couldn't be further from the truth.

The problem is that with a shift to more instructional time and test preparation, our academic performance hasn't improved, but rather it has steadily declined. Even though we spend more money, use more technology, and focus more on standardized testing than ever before, the result is we still trail most other industrialized countries in student achievement. While there are many factors that may contribute to the decline in international ranking, education has apparently missed the mark with the measures we currently use. For example, can you guess what countries like Finland, where students have recess multiple times throughout the day, or Singapore, where they use technology sparingly in the classroom, have in common? They all dominate us on international testing. Most of our schools won't even allow recess or play time, because it's seen as a waste of time since it takes away from learning. However, we will learn in this book that the breaks, play, and physical activity are an integral part of learning and actually help the brain retain and process information more effectively. In fact, children lack certain development skills simply because they lack coordination, balance, and core strength.

In May 2011, Kathryn L. King, MD, and Carly J. Scahill, DO, from the Medical University of South Carolina Children's Hospital, released a study of 1st- through 6th-graders at an academically low-performing elementary school in Charleston, SC. The researchers found that, after the students participated in 40 minutes of activity each day, five days a week (as opposed to their usual 40 minutes per week), the number of students who reached proficiency on the year-end state tests improved from 55 percent to 68.5 percent. Could you imagine test scores improving this dramatically from simply getting your students moving and active?

Unfortunately, when our students perform below average, we cut out their recess or take them out of classes like physical education to give them more remedial work. Then we wonder why students dread or even hate coming to school. In essence, we have childproofed education, because children are naturally active and inquisitive beings, yet we expect them to sit for hours and learn. We will repeat this statement throughout the book, but it bears repeating: the sedentary nature of education is the greatest disservice we have done to children in the last 50 years!

With the rise in sedentary obesity, ADD, ADHD, and other issues, education has becomes more like *"meducation,"* where we insensitively tell parents that their children are obese and where any traits like fidgeting or high energy have to be a medical issue. No one has taken a moment to realize that some of the fidgeting and restlessness could simply be a result of sedentary education. We are aware one of the issues is that teachers have so much pressure to document and justify what they do and why they do it, that the relaxed playful environment is compromised. But effective teachers will do what is best for the kid's sake, while trying to fit into the ever-growing restraints they must work within.

Formal education has to make serious transformations if we ever hope to improve student health, behavior, and, just as importantly, achievement. In *Learning on Your Feet: Incorporating Physical Activity into the K-8 Classroom*, we provide an abundance of evidence to support the need for a dramatic transformation of the classroom. Everything from the design of the classroom to managing a more active classroom is included. We discuss how STEM classes need to be more real-world and physically engaging as well as how we need to shut off the computers more, or at least make technology use more active as well.

What makes this book stand out from traditional classroom books is the inclusion of more physical fitness, which research shows dramatically improves students' focus, behavior, and achievement. But understand that the research and activities aren't just an extension of physical education class. Rather, they focus on developing core, balance, and fitness, which improve reading, critical thinking, organization, focus, behavior, and overall academic achievement. The research in this book overwhelmingly reinforces our position that a fit body is critical to maximum student achievement and overall success. What is interesting is that many academic issues with reading or math are actually often related to physical issues. For example, as we will discuss in the book, poor reading skills may in some part be attributed to lack of coordination (body midline), which impedes the ability to read from left to right.

I (Melody) have spent years working with the general population, especially children, on functional training and have seen how most people lack core strength and coordination. Core strength helps students focus, improve behavior, and achievement because it helps develop the part of the brain where these executive functions occur. Balance or coordination is another area where students, even athletes, show a lack of development. I have trained athletes who were in good muscular shape, but still lacked core strength, and coordination.

When I work with schools on concepts such as balance, teachers will often think the athletic children will perform well, but the reality is that they typically have underdeveloped coordination skills, not just poor core development. When students lose focus in class, slump over their desks, or seem to be daydreaming, these issues can sometimes be linked to poor core development. Poor core strength affects the area of the brain that controls executive function, which is responsible for mental focus, organization, and processing information. So, if this area is underdeveloped, then students have even more problems with lack of focus, fidgeting, and ultimately achievement. Most educators don't fully understand the relationship between the body and the mind. A strong body helps create a strong mind. Students that I have worked with not only improve in their physical performance, but their parents let me know they perform better in schools as well. When I got this feedback consistently from parents, I knew this information needed to be shared, with teachers and parents alike.

Fortunately there are simple exercises and activities that can be included in the classroom which can help significantly improve the core and balance of students so that they can remain focused, engaged, and finish the day with high energy. The strategies can be implemented for individual students or the whole class.

If the ideas and strategies in this book are implemented into the traditional classroom, you will see a significant change in your students' behavior, productivity, sense of well-being, and achievement. Students' achievement can increase dramatically as their overall fitness improves. Teachers have also greatly benefited from the exercises discussed in this book, with weight loss, improved core strength, balance, and increased sense of well-being. Every chapter has great ideas to try, so feel free to implement as few or as many as you feel comfortable including in your classroom.

As Texas A&M Professor Dr. Mark Benden shared in our interview, "We will look back over the past generation and wonder what were we thinking? Making students sit and learn all day. It goes against their very nature." As an educator for the past two decades, I (Brad) agree wholeheartedly and believe it is time to make public education effective again by getting students to Learn on Their Feet!

Acknowledgments

Special thanks to the following contributors to the book:

Aleta Margolis, founder of Inspired Teaching

Vera O'Sullivan, photographer, exercise photos and cover photo

Shannon Miller, Olympic gold medal in gymnastics, child health advocate

Angela Hanscom, Pediatric Occupational Therapist, founder of Timbernook

Dr. Mark Benden, Professor at Texas A&M

Rae Pica, educational consultant, education radio host

Dr. Marilyn Wedge, child and family therapist

Rebeca Plantier, founder of Fit to Inspire, writer for Huffington Post

Dr. Spyridoula Vazou, Assistant Professor of Exercise Psychology and Pedagogy in the Department of Kinesiology at Iowa State University

Jamie Shankles, founder of Niyelo: adventure-based therapy and outdoor education

Jeremy Johnson, BS in Wellness, ACSM certified trainer

Introduction

Why Do Students Need to Get Moving More?

We Learn Better on Our Feet than in Our Seats

Exercise is Miracle-Gro for the brain.

John Ratey (author, professor Harvard University)

As the quote suggests, exercise really is Miracle-Gro for the brain. Regular physical activity supports healthy child development by improving memory, concentration, and positive outlook. The connection between learning and exercise seems to be especially strong for elementary school students. Given these findings and the ones which will be discussed throughout this book, cutting back on physical education, recess, and even play with the aim of improving academic performance, as some districts have done, appears to be counterproductive.

The fact is that children learn better when they are active and engaged. Unfortunately, public education in a sense has "childproofed" education. Think of how all young animals learn. They learn through movement, play, and exploration. You don't see a bear cub learning how to eat and survive by sitting still, just as you don't see a baby learning by laying still. In fact, young babies are so active that some young parents actually childproof their homes with locks, latchets, and other barriers so their children won't get injured or harmed while exploring. Similarly, education has childproofed education as well. Students are expected to sit quietly in their desks all day without opportunities to explore, play, and move. When we cut out or remove recess, physical education, and other opportunities for children to learn in the manner in which they are designed to learn.

As **Dr. Mark Benden** (professor at Texas A&M) shared in our interview, "We will look back on the past generation and ask, 'What were those people thinking making children sit still all day in school. Who thought that was a good idea?' It's probably the *greatest disservice* we have done to children in this past generation. Children need to be moving and active. One has to look no further than the rise in sedentary epidemic obesity, ADD, and ADHD to see a correlation between their increase and inactivity in the classroom."

Dr. Benden's research in pilot schools, as well as other research, shows that exercise has both a physiological and developmental impact on children's brains. Physical mechanisms include: increased oxygen to the brain, change in bloodstream composition, alterations to neurotransmitters, and structural changes in the central nervous system that enhance the brains ability to learn. So, incorporating short exercise or stretch breaks into lessons can re-sharpen children's focus on learning. Especially for younger students, dividing lessons into 10- to 20-minute "chunks" highlighted with activities that involve movement keeps their attention on learning and helps make the content more memorable. Exercise and stretch breaks also work well during transitions between lessons. The mind works best when the body is involved. Remember: children by nature are active beings.

Education has become so focused on testing that we forgot how children actually learn. The problem is that a focus on testing, rather than on how children learn, has caused a steady decline in academic achievement, along with a plethora of other issues. As **Dr. Marilyn Wedge** (therapist, author) explained:

We can learn from other countries. In Finland, for example, where students continually outperform American kids on respected international tests (PISA tests), for every 45 minutes of class time children get 15 minutes of recess. In Finnish elementary schools, the school day is only 4 hours long, and children are encouraged to participate in sports after school.

Reducing or eliminating homework and encouraging children to ride bikes, participate in sports, or socialize with their friends after school is another good way to get kids more active. Jane Hsu, principal of a New York City elementary school, has banned all homework from her school. According to this principal, research has shown that homework has negative effects on children. Homework can cause kids to become frustrated and lose interest in learning, and they can miss out on activities with family and friends.

In areas where it is appropriate and safe, parents can walk to school with their kids. Research has shown that just 20 minutes of walking to school can help a child focus better in the classroom. First, physical activity improves brain elasticity, which allows children to learn more easily. Second, there is evidence that contact with the natural environment has a calming effect on children. And third, exercise also releases endorphins (neurotransmitters that produce a feeling of well-being), which makes children feel more relaxed.

Olympic gold medalist and education advocate **Shannon Miller** shared her views on active learning in a recent interview with us. As she explained,

It's critical on so many levels to get our kids active throughout the day, particularly at a young age. Physical activity helps them focus better during class, sleep better at night, maintain a healthy weight, and combat the risks of type 2 diabetes and cardiovascular disease. It helps with self-esteem and confidence, and it gives children an opportunity to find a sport or activity they are passionate about. The list of benefits goes on and on. As we see physical education being cut from school curriculum, we have to look for ways to keep our children active. Ten-minute 'brain breaks' can go a long way. That time can be used to incorporate physical activity with a learning activity like math and vocabulary. It can be as creative as you like or as simple as having the kids get up and dance. The goal is 60 minutes of physical activity but we've seen increased brain function with something as simple as a 20-minute walk.

The importance of getting children active from a young age cannot be stressed enough. When children are active early in life, they tend to remain active for a lifetime.

As most of us realize, formal education is no longer an active process. Children sit in desks or even in groups and listen to lectures and work on assignments with very little physical activity involved. Think about it: the major focal point of work during a school day is the students seated at their desk. From kindergarten through high school, students spend most of their academic lives in a desk. It seems almost inhumane if you think about the amount of time we subject children to a seated position.

Beyond health, there is also research to suggest that how we educate may be the reason that students' creativity and intelligence is hindered through their informative years. We have all heard of Gardner's multiple intelligences, but you may not be familiar with some of the results of his work. In one longitudinal study, Gardner found that children up to the age of 4 in a group were all operating at the genius level, while the same group of children at age 20 dropped to only 10 percent operating at the genius level. So, what happened between the age of 4 and 20 that would cause such a drop in genius level? Well, frankly, public education happened. Until the age of 4, children are constantly moving, playing, and learning in a state of constant motion. But when they enter school, the focus becomes on uniformity, control, following rules, sitting in a desk, and the list goes on. This study reinforces our research that we are shortchanging our students when it comes to overall education and student achievement. So, you may ask, what is it about movement and learning that is so important anyway?

First, physical activity improves brain elasticity, which allows children to learn more easily. Second, there is evidence that contact with the natural environment has a calming effect on children. And third, exercise also releases endorphins (neurotransmitters that produce a feeling of wellbeing), which makes children feel more relaxed. Finally, the brain processes movement in the same part of the brain that processes learning. So, if students are sitting still then the learning process is actually hindered, rather than enhanced.

Studies provide evidence that many years of fine motor exercise allows brain reorganization and nerve growth. Physical movement such as standing, stretching, walking, or marching can help the brain focus better. For instance, if students feel drowsy, they should be allowed to stand at the back of the room for up to two minutes and stretch on their own. I (Brad) remember when I taught middle grades science—I would always have the students moving. Even when taking notes, I would let the students stand by their desks, sit on the floor, or even lie on the floor. If a student had too much energy, I would let them go to the back of the class and do pushups. Students quickly adapt to these situations, so that there are very little behavior issues, because this becomes the norm for the classroom. The change in levels and body positions help develop the vestibular system (inner ear and balance) as well as their core muscles, which we will discuss in detail later in the book.

Dr. Spyridoula Vazou (Professor at Iowa State University) shared her expertise in the area of active learning in the classroom. As she stated,

> Yes, the weight of the evidence suggests that there is a benefit from both acute (immediate benefit) and chronic (long-term participation) physical activity and exercise on cognition and, in turn, on academic performance. Physical activity is not antagonistic to learning. To the contrary, it helps learning. Therefore, the oxymoron of cutting time from recess, playtime and physical activity in order to focus on academic performance needs to change.
>
> In addition to recess and PE, a very promising and attractive approach to helping students be more physically active is adding short (about five-minute) activity breaks (e.g., stand and march, stretch, or jump in place) in the classroom and throughout the school day. That way, students are not distracted from their lesson and, at the same time, they are being physically active. Research shows that, by adding movement in the classroom (either as activity breaks or in integration with academics), students can get about 19 additional minutes of physical activity daily. Accumulating short bouts of activity throughout the day can help students stay focused and, at the same time, meet the recommended guidelines for physical activity (60 minutes of moderate to vigorous physical activity daily).

Movement should be an important part of the school day, as movement can influence the brains of students. Most neuroscientists agree that there is a connection between movement and cognition or learning. Movement should be a part of all subject areas of the curriculum. Physical activities like role-playing, doing hands-on activities such as math manipulatives, are more likely to be recalled. When we keep students active, we keep their energy levels up and provide their brains with the oxygen-rich blood needed for highest performance. Equally important, though perhaps less obvious, is movement for learning in the early school years is because the executive function system in the brain is developing rapidly.

We will discuss the executive function more in a later chapter, but it is responsible for abilities such as setting goals, planning, focusing attention, and thinking abstractly—precisely the components needed for success in school. A growing body of research demonstrates the connection between physical activity and enhanced EF in children. This means active students tend to focus and function better.

Children enter school with enthusiasm and a sense of wonder, which can enhance their desire to learn and excel. They naturally learn through exploration, play, creativity, and, yes, even hard work. But too often these traits are not reinforced, because they aren't thought to be necessary to pass a standardized test. We focus more on students walking in lines, sitting in desks, and working quietly. We must remember that children learn through many mediums, which can actually involve playing, moving, and having fun. Brain-based research emphasizes that learning is enhanced when children are moving and active.

Have you ever wondered why children start school with "wide-eyed wonder" and excitement, but soon it almost becomes a boring routine? It is often because we remove the curiosity of learning by limiting the ability of students to be active and engaged. Children leave a home structure where they can play, move, and explore. They enter school and now they are expected to sit for most of the day. Could you imagine having a classroom where students come in every day excited and ready to learn because they know they will get to play, move, and explore? This description of this behavior is a far cry from many classrooms, where students sit still and memorize fragmented bits of information. What a contradiction to their inquisitive and exploring nature.

For many teachers this type of teaching calls for a paradigm shift in classroom management. Giving up some control of the classroom to allow for play and exploration can be a scary and challenging task. Will the students learn? Will they perform well on tests? Will they meet all of the curriculum standards? You may be hesitant to step outside your comfort zone and try a new approach, so our goal is to help you begin with simple changes within your comfort level, and, as you see the success, then you will be willing to make more changes. Just imagine if these changes allowed students the freedom to move, play, and maintain their creativity. What if 30 or 40 percent of your students left school still functioning at a genius level? Your students would thank you for making a difference in their lives.

Finally, there is overwhelming research to suggest that physical activity not only helps with student focus, improved behavior, and remaining on task, but the research shows that physical activity does improve standardized test scores. And let's face it—standardized test scores are the driving force of education, so why not improve those scores as well?

In one study, reported in the *Journal of Pediatrics* (Rauner et al., 2013), research showed that physical activity was more important than even weight status in determining standardized test scores in math and reading. The study examined 12,000 Nebraska students' timed runs and BMIs against their standardized test scores. The researchers found that higher levels of aerobic fitness corresponded with better academic performance. Interestingly, a child's weight or BMI didn't matter—it was their level of physical fitness that corresponded to the better scores. In fact, the data showed that physical fitness was a significant predictor of academic performance even in students who may be overweight. This means that increasing physical activity is important for improving academics.

Another study, *The Influence of Childhood Aerobic Fitness on Learning and Memory* focused on cognitive function for tasks requiring perception, memory, and cognitive control. They had students memorize fictitious names and locations and measured the success based upon fitness levels. Students who were in the high fitness group scored higher than the students in the low fitness group. When asked to remember the locations after straight memorization, the fit kids scored an average of 43 percent. The unfit kids scored an average 25.8 percent.

Finally, a study published in *Developmental Neuroscience* was carried out with 9- to 10-year-old students in Chicago. The researchers sorted the children into highest and lowest fitness categories based upon treadmill testing. Both groups completed a series of cognitive challenges involving watching directional arrows on a computer screen and pushing certain keys in order to test how well the children filter out unnecessary information and attend to relevant cues. Finally, the children's brains were scanned, using magnetic resonance imaging (MRI) technology to measure the volume of specific areas.

The students from the highest fitness group performed better on the tests. MRI tests showed that certain parts of the fitness group's brains (that help with memory and focus) were more developed as well. Since both groups of children had similar socioeconomic backgrounds, body mass index and other variables, the researchers concluded that being fit had enlarged that portion of their brains.

Unfortunately, with initiatives like No Child Left Behind (NCLB) and such a focus on standardized testing, we have removed recess, physical education, and many opportunities for students to be active and move in the classroom. All for the sake of better test scores. The irony is that an inactive environment actually hinders achievement, and we see this in the continual drop of the USA in international tests scores such as PISA.

The research in this chapter and throughout the book is overwhelming—active students perform better on standardized tests than do sedentary students. Active students are more engaged, on task, and perform better academically. The problem is that we have been trained to think that education should focus only on the brain, which can be detrimental to the well-being as well as academic achievement of our students. As Dr. Benden suggested, we are doing our students a great disservice and it's time to rethink what are truly the best practices to maximize student achievement by getting their minds and bodies in motion!

Key Points to Remember

- The brain works best when it is used in tandem with the body. The mind and body in motion together create an optimal learning environment.

- Children are designed to be moving and active.

- Active and fit children perform better academically.

- Exercise releases endorphins, which make children feel better and relax, too.

- Multiple intelligences, and even genius, are magnified through movement and creative learning.

- Exercise is like Miracle-Gro for the brain.

- Sedentary education is the greatest disservice we have done to children in the last generation!

Getting Started

Preparing to Incorporate Movement in the Classroom

2 | Transforming the Physical Classroom

"The classroom should no longer be centered around the student desk."

Brad Johnson

Education has adapted to culture in the sense that we now use technology such as smartboards, computers, and even LCD projectors in the classroom. But beyond technology, classrooms have changed very little in the past century. Walk into any classroom and you will find a teacher's desk, teacher's table, and 20–40 student desks. The student desk is where most of the day is spent by students. It is almost like their little room away from home. However, as we suggest throughout the book, students need to move and be active, not simply sit in desks all day. Ironically, I have never seen a desk where students sit all day at home. It seems we have it backwards, because students should spend more time standing and moving than they should sitting.

A change in the physical classroom can also be beneficial to teachers. How many teachers spend their time walking around the room, bent over talking to students at their desks? Now, how many of those teachers leave at the end of the day with their backs sore or hurting? Yes, many or most of them. So, if sitting is not the most effective way to learn, as the research throughout the book suggests, then maybe it is time for a classroom make-over. Maybe it's time to actually design a classroom to suit the needs of the learners. When you attend a fitness center, it is designed to meet the needs of the members; when you eat out, the restaurant will be designed for the best dining experience possible. Classrooms aren't designed to maximize learning. They are designed to maximize control.

A lot of interaction in the classroom should be team-building activities as we discuss in Chapter 7. However, the traditional classroom is not conducive to that type of learning. Interestingly, the corporate world has adapted to the need of more movement, interaction, and a change in how their physical worlds look. Many corporations have done makeovers and removed the traditional cubicles with a desk. Kraft Corporation, for example, has generated a philosophy that promotes teamwork and sustainability. To make this shift, Kraft has redesigned buildings and altered the culture within the workplace. Kraft had traditional office spaces for years, with the plush, expansive, executive offices on their own floor and floor after floor of closed-off cubicles, office, and cubbies. Kraft was structured like most traditional companies across the world. That type of environment did not promote engagement and interaction.

One top vice president for Kraft said that people would walk by her office and never come in to talk. They would send her an email instead of face-to-face conversations. She recognized that this culture needed to change and was in support of the multi-million-dollar renovation of the facilities. Kraft made a conscious effort to create a paradigm shift of removing the hierarchical structure and creating an "open space" concept. There were several goals associated with the open space concept, which included sustainability, collaboration, and creating a culture of teamwork. She says that now people walk up to her and engage in conversation and share ideas. The entire culture of the company has changed to promote collaboration and teamwork, because the work space is more conducive to interaction rather than working in isolation.

Beyond these changes, corporations have taken it even further by incorporating fitness equipment as office furniture. Many corporations have exchanged traditional desks and chairs with stand-up desks, stability ball chairs, and even treadmills with stand-up workstations, so employees can actually walk in place while they work. Dr. Benden (professor at Texas A&M) is a leading expert in the field of ergonomics (design intended to provide optimum comfort and to avoid stress or injury). He has worked with large corporations such as Johnson & Johnson on incorporating physical changes into the workplace to improve productivity and health benefits of employees. Dr. Benden's research has focused on Technology Induced Inactivity and the manner in which our sedentary lifestyles are increasingly influencing poor health outcomes, obesity and type 2 diabetes. Central to this effort has been adult- and child-focused research that evaluates his concept of a stand-based workstation to increase physical activity. He took this technology and developed the standing desk and workstations which can be seen in this chapter. His research with pilot school programs is noted throughout the book.

Another option is active workstations. A growing number of Americans are standing, walking, and even cycling, their way through the workday at treadmill desks, stand-up desks, or other moving workstations. Others are forgoing chairs in favor of giant exercise balls to stay fit. Treadmill desks designed for the workplace are normally set to move at 1–2 mph, enough to get the heart rate up, but not too fast to distract from reading or talking on the phone comfortably. "It's been a decade since scientific studies began to show that too much sitting can lead to obesity and increase the risk of developing diabetes, high blood pressure and heart disease. Even going to the gym three times a week doesn't offset the harm of being sedentary for hours at a time," said **Dr. James Levine**, an endocrinologist at the Mayo Clinic.

Several schools around the country and internationally have already begun to make transformations to the classroom, such as adding treadmills and stationary bikes. One such class is at Ward Elementary School in North Carolina. They have a classroom with enough stationary bikes for each student. They call it the read and ride program. Teachers can bring their students to the classroom throughout the day and let them read while riding stationary bikes. When they analyzed data at the end of school year, they found that students who had spent the most time in the read and ride program achieved an 83 percent proficiency in reading, while those who spent the least amount of time in the program had failing scores, with only 41 percent proficiency.

Scott Ertl is the teacher who started the program at the school. As he has explained in interviews, "Riding exercise bikes makes reading fun for many kids who get frustrated when they read. They have a way to release that frustration they feel while they ride." This type of exercise is also great for students who may be overweight and not enjoy physical education. It allows them to work at their own pace without worrying about what classmates think, since they are busy riding and reading themselves. The program has already expanded in more than 30 other schools in the area, and more schools around the country are implementing similar programs. Students, no matter their grade, age, or disability, have one thing in common: they can read and ride!

While the design of the classroom needs to, and has to, change to fully engage and benefit the students, the learning experience needs to expand beyond the four walls of the physical classroom. As the old adage goes, the world is a classroom. In my first year teaching, I was asked to co-teach an outdoor education course. It was not anything that I had been prepared to teach during my teacher education program. But it was an incredible experience that was very different than the traditional classroom.

The class mainly took place outdoors, where the students would work on team-building, leadership, and critical thinking skills. The beauty of the course was that all of the initiatives and activities were all physical in nature. There were no desk, no note taking, and no students who were bored. This was typically the one class that students looked forward to each day. Some of the activities were pretty physical, but it was up to the team to make sure everyone was successful. Students left this course with better interpersonal skills, better focus on learning, and improved achievement through improved critical thinking. I have to admit that the class not only positively affected the students, but as a teacher it influenced how I taught core subject areas like science for the rest of my teaching career.

I know of several programs in Canada and in Europe where students are outside all day long. You may think that weather would prohibit going outside, but I love the attitude of one site director that said there is no such thing as poor weather, just poor clothing choices. One of the first in Canada opened its doors, or rather its gates, in around 2010. The Carp Ridge Forest Pre-School offers its students few comforts like toys, climate control, or electric power in Ottawa's rural western outskirts. Instead, it boasts a garden, trails through the woods, and a tentlike shelter called a yurt, and aims to help children aged 3 to 6 to connect with nature.

In the UK and throughout Europe these are known as forest kindergartens. While this may conjure up images of Hansel and Gretel, the students do much more than walk around the woods all day. Because the activities are not manufactured by toys, prefab games, or other curriculum, students are involved in more authentic learning. Many of the noted benefits of this vigorous program include improved skills, such as: constructive contributions to learning, asking questions and interest in learning, motivation, sports, music, art and creativity, and even positive social behavior. Imagine if we moved beyond the walls of the classroom and brought the passion and invigoration of the real world back to learning.

Ideas to Try

- **Stand-up desk** (Stand2Learn™). The rise of the standing desk may appear to be a response to the modern, eat-at-your-desk, hunched-over worker chained to her computer, but did you know that people like Benjamin

Franklin and Thomas Jefferson stood while they worked. Workplaces are moving toward more standing desks, but schools have been slower to catch on for a variety of reasons, including cost, convenience, and perhaps the traditional beliefs that "sit down and pay attention" is the best way to learn.

The research comes more from observing the health results of people's behavior than from discovering the biological and genetic triggers that may be associated with extended sitting. Research such as Dr. Benden's (professor Texas A&M) has determined that, after an hour or more of sitting, the production of enzymes that burn fat in the body declines by as much as 90 percent. Extended sitting, they add, slows the body's metabolism of glucose and lowers the levels of good (HDL) cholesterol in the blood. Those are risk factors toward developing heart disease and type 2 diabetes. Dr. Benden has actually helped patent several pieces of equipment that are being used in schools, such as the stand-up desk. What makes this desk unique, if you look at the picture, is that it has a built-in foot pedal at the base of the desk. The foot pedal allows a student to actually pump the pedal when he or she gets too much nervous energy without interrupting the entire class. Because it is below the line of sight, most students won't even know when it is being used.

- **Stability ball chairs.** Stability balls have been known to help strengthen the core. However, there is the potential to fall off stability balls, and some experts feel they may not be the best option for safety reasons. However, the stability ball chair provides more stability and safety, while still strengthening the core. Gather everyone on the rug, and make the introduction. Explain that they are important pieces of equipment that are to be used properly, that they will help you sit up straight, have strong core muscles, and even help you focus. Model how to sit on the ball correctly (feet flat on the floor at "10 o'clock" and "2 o'clock," back straight) and how, while sitting, you can very lightly bounce and swivel while you are working, without leaning. Give every child a chance to sit on the ball for a few seconds. Explain where and when they can sit on the balls. The students will be curious as to who gets the balls at what time. If you don't have enough chairs for each student, simply create a rotation log. For instance, if you can afford four chairs, then rotate four students using the chairs each day. However, if you can find grant money, support of parents, PTO, or other methods, maybe you can supply the entire class!

- **Kinesthetic active student workstations**: Similar to the workstations used in corporations, the kinesthetic workstation engages a variety of muscle groups and promotes collaboration as students' transition between active movements. The workstation is different than the stand-up desk because it allows for up to six students to work at the same table. The standing kinesthetic desk includes 1 stand-and-sway station, 1 pedal station, 2 stand and spin stations, and 2 balance stations. Seated Kinesthetic Desk includes 2 pedal seats, 2 kneeling seats, and 2 pogo seats for great variety. These would be great for any classroom or lab class.

- **Disc'O'Sit**. The Disc'O'Sit is a round dynamic cushion with one bumpy side and one smooth side. It offers "active sitting," which strengthens the muscles that support the spine. Use when a greater range of motion and sensory input is needed. Very helpful for decreasing fidgeting and increasing awareness. Can be used in a variety of other ways, including for floor activities and/or in conjunction with a ball to promote strength, balance, and sensory integration. It can also be used for standing activities and even in hydrotherapy for flotation. Inflate to desired level. Making a few cushions available for anyone who wants them will allow children who really need them to gravitate toward them without feeling singled out.

- **Fitness area.** One way to ensure that students have an area to burn off some excess energy is to create a fitness center in your classroom. We have reading centers and math centers, so why not have a fitness center? In this area you can have items such as BOSU balls, stability balls, steps, and much more. This can be an area where students can come and exercise for a few minutes during class if they feel too fidgety. Or you may use the area to do circuit exercises with your entire class. Many classrooms around the country are starting to add fitness equipment such as treadmills and stationary bikes to their classrooms as well. In fact some teachers use a stationary bike as a behavior management tool. When students get too fidgety, they are allowed to go to the back of the class and ride on the bike. Then they return to their seat and resume class. This type of set up keeps students focused, engaged, and keeps them from losing recess or other privileges.

Key Points to Remember

- Classrooms don't need to look like they did 50 years ago. Create an active classroom with equipment to keep students active.

- Create a fitness area where fidgety students can exercise without disrupting the entire class.

- Use the outdoors as your extended classroom.

- Use grants, resources, or even the PTO, to help fund items such as stability ball chairs.

- Make the room conducive to team-building opportunities.

- Get students out of their desks as much as possible.

Integrating Fitness and Technology

3

"*Use technology to promote movement, not inhibit it.*"

Brad Johnson

Probably the greatest change in education over the past 30 years has been the use of technology. As late as the 1990s, there was still not much technology in the average classroom. There were typing and computer classes, but personal computers, laptops, and iPads weren't commonplace yet. However, one of the biggest challenges we now face with the use of technology is the sedentary nature of sitting and working on a computer. It is the same dilemma as sitting at a desk all day, but now you have a piece of electronic equipment that makes it more enjoyable to sit and play.

So, in some aspects, technology has actually helped create the sedentary learning environment that exists in education. Even though videogames began to enter homes during the 1970s and 1980s, children still spent plenty of time outdoors playing play catch, freeze tag, hide and seek, or riding bikes, which provided adequate physical exercise. Being stuck in the house was like a punishment to the average kid during this time. However, today, with videogames, cell phones, iPads, personal computers, and 400 channels of television, children spend about seven hours per day in the virtual world.

While technology has improved civilization, maybe too much of a good thing has started to cause some unwanted side effects. For instance, since the 1980s childhood obesity has nearly tripled. And is sitting in front of a computer monitor really stimulating the brain and enhancing achievement like we first thought? Research by Lin and Zhou (2012), as reported in *Psychology Today*, showed that excessive use of technology like surfing the internet and videogames actually causes atrophy in the frontal lobe of the brain. If you recall, this is the same area of the brain that affects ADD and ADHD. It is the area that governs executive functions, such as planning, prioritizing, organizing, and impulse control. So, maybe one of the unintended consequences of too much hard-wired technology is less hard-wired gray matter?

So, excessive screen time appears to impair brain structure and function. Much of the damage occurs in the brain's frontal lobe, which undergoes massive changes from youth until the mid-twenties. Frontal lobe development, in turn, largely determines success in every area of life, from sense of well-being to academic or career success and even relationship skills.

Not only does excessive technology reduce the size of our brains, but it increases the waistline of our students as well as lowering fitness levels. A number of research studies have shown a relationship between screen time and increased risk for childhood obesity. A November 2012 Australian study of 9- to 16-year-old children published in *Acta Paediatrica* found that more than two hours of screen time (computer and television) per day significantly increased the risk for being overweight and obese. The sedentary nature of surfing the internet or using laptops is not just about weight gain, but about decreasing fitness levels. As we mentioned in Chapter 1, students' achievement was tied to level of fitness more so than BMI (body mass index). So, active children tend to learn better.

In *The Smartest Kids in the World*, Amanda Ripley describes three school settings in South Korea, Finland, and Poland as being devoid of the technology that we take for granted in the USA, and how, especially in math and science, their best students outperform our best students by a wide margin. As the Minister of Education and Science at the Finnish Parliament, **Krista Kiuru** explains, "Finnish students and teachers didn't need laptops and iPads to get to the top of international education rankings ... And officials aren't interested in using them to stay there." This is in glaring contrast to the US, where the current administration believes that technology is critical for improving schools. While technology is an important tool, the debate and focus of its importance really does detract from the real issues of educating students. Remember this top-performing country may not overindulge in technology for their students, so why do we see it as the savior of education?

Speaking of overindulgence, did you know that the term *internet use disorder*, or *internet addiction disorder*, was added to the 2013 edition of the *Diagnostic and Statistical Manual of Mental Disorders* (DSM) for further study? In order to be added to the manual, research had to demonstrate not only that screen time can become a regular habit that has the potential to disrupt daily life, but also that there is neurological evidence to back up that claim. Internet addiction is considered to be part of a broader "technology addiction." In fact, children are exposed to more information by the age of 5 than their grandparents were by the age of 18. With children being inundated with information, do they know how to process it properly? Do they know what to tune into and what to tune out of? Maybe one of the reasons other countries perform better is that their students don't have a lot of technology cluttering their minds and interrupting their ability to process important information.

Other research suggests that too much computer use actually has a negative effect on student achievement. The Organization for Economic Cooperation and Development (OECD), who is actually responsible for PISA (Program for International Student Assessment) testing, examined computer use among 15-year-olds across 31 nations and regions, and found that students who used computers more at school had both *lower* reading and *lower* math scores, as measured by PISA.

"Those who use the internet every day do the worst," said **Andreas Schleicher**, OECD Director for Education and author of "Students, Computers and Learning: Making the Connection," the OECD's first report to look at the digital skills of students around the world. Some of the key findings from the report include:

- Students who use computers very frequently at school get worse results.
- Students who use computers moderately at school, such as once or twice a week, have "somewhat better learning outcomes" than students who use computers rarely.
- The results show "no appreciable improvements" in reading, mathematics, or science in the countries that had invested heavily in information technology.
- High-achieving school systems such as South Korea and Shanghai in China have lower levels of computer use in school.
- Singapore, with only a moderate use of technology in school, is top for digital skills.
- One of the most disappointing findings of the report is that the socio-economic divide between students is not narrowed by technology, perhaps even amplified.

The study revealed that home computer use, by contrast, wasn't as harmful to academic achievement. Students in many high-performing nations reported spending between one to two hours a day on a computer outside of school. Across the 31 nations and regions, the average 15-year-old spent more than two hours a day on the computer. However, the study found that, in the classroom, school systems with more computers tended to improve less. Those with fewer computers were seeing larger educational gains, as measured by PISA test score changes between 2009 and 2012. "One of the most disappointing findings of the report is that the socio-economic divide between students is not narrowed by technology, perhaps even amplified," said Mr. Schleicher. He further stated, "Making sure all children have a good grasp of reading and math is a more effective way to close the gap than access to hi-tech devices."

When it comes to changes in education, very little persuades us without data to show it affects student achievement. In fact, among the seven countries with the highest level of internet use in school, it found three experienced "significant declines" in reading performance (Australia, New Zealand, and Sweden)—and three more had results that showed no improvement in scores (Spain, Norway, and Denmark).

With this research coming from the OECD, it is apparent that computers and technology in the classroom isn't the magic formula some believed it to be and it reinforces what I have always known to be true: that nothing takes the place of an effective teacher in the classroom. Since achievement is often our main concern in education, and since this study was done by the organization that actually created the PISA, its data should at least cause us to reflect on how much technology we incorporate versus the amount of time students should be actively learning.

While technology does serve an important purpose in our lives and in education, it is critical that we focus on incorporating activity with technology use to help offset some of the negative effects sedentary use and overuse. With a little creativity and innovation, you can actually integrate technology and physical activity in the classroom to make the best use of both worlds. Remember: technology adds to the sedentary nature of learning, so we have to begin with changing how we deliver technology. Even videogame companies are aware that this type of entertainment can cause children to be too sedentary. So, being ahead of the curve, they have created games like the Wii, Xbox Kinect, and other games that require movement. Even the gaming industry understands that sitting for long periods is unhealthy. In fact, Kinect-EDucation is an educator-driven community resource for developers, teachers, students, enthusiasts, and any other education stakeholder to promote the use of Kinect applications in classrooms. With Kinect, students can actively engage in concepts such as virtual piano, exploring anatomy, robotics, manipulate drawings, navigation, and many more ideas that can be found on their website (www.kinecteducation.com). Studies have indicated that active gaming can promote higher levels of energy expenditure compared to seated videogames, as well as increasing heart rate and oxygen consumption.

With all the technology at the tip of our fingers, surely we can find ways to include it in making classrooms more active for children. And, when we do use technology, remember to incorporate active movement to ensure that the students are keeping the mind and body in motion. Physical education programs, for example, do a good job of incorporating technology with fitness. Pedometers are becoming commonplace in many elementary physical education classes and students are starting to use them all day long, not just in physical education. Dr. Benden, a professor at Texas A&M who has done much research in the area, believes that we need to use technology to help us get more active rather than using it in a sedentary manner. He likes the use of pedometers, heart-rate monitors, and other devices that allow students to gauge their energy expenditure and fitness levels. One idea he would like to see is some kind of monitor or device, such as an app, that will vibrate and alert the user when they have been sedentary too long. This would be beneficial to teachers as well, because it could be set to let them know when it's time to take a brain break!

Integrating technology with fitness should also be a focus for the overall health of our students. Adults now use technology in the form of apps and web-based programs to help them with their fitness and nutritional goals. Therefore, programs could be set up to help students understand their health and well-being better, as well. With apps, students can keep track of their daily calorie expenditures as well as the number of calories they consume each day. This can help students better understand the importance of being active and physically fit.

For example, students could use apps to determine the amount of exercise necessary to burn off calories associated with certain foods like a candy bar. For instance, there are 250 calories in a Snickers bar. So, students could use apps, pedometers, or other technology to figure out how much exercise is required to burn off the 215 calories. For example, jogging for 20 minutes will burn about 200 calories. Playing an active game on Wii for 50 minutes will burn about 200 calories as well. While these are a few examples, allow students to find other ways to burn 200–215 calories and then let the class participate in the activities. I can guarantee you that once they realize how much exercise is involved, they will never look at a candy bar the same way again!

Finally, it's also OK to let students be creative when it comes to technology and fitness. Teacher and author **Vicki Davis**, host of one of the top education radio programs, *Every Classroom Matters*, shared with us that she integrates technology and physical activity in the classroom by having students invent games. Then they actually go outside or in the gym and play the games. They incorporate technology by keeping stats, charts, etc. from the game and then use them in programs such as Excel to track data, calories burned, and other information that can be used for both math and science.

Ideas to Try

- **SMART board fitness games.** The SMART board is a great resource for integrating physical activity into your learning. On the most basic level, SMART boards can get students up, walking to the board, and stretching as they move elements around the board.

  One activity allows students to throw a beanbag or koosh ball at the marker on the screen to open the next question. In this example, there are also physical activity examples that students can mimic as a classroom warmup or fitness break.

- **Activity trackers and pedometers.** An activity tracker (also called an accelerometer) is an instrument generally worn on either the trunk or limbs that measures duration, frequency, and intensity of physical activity; this measurement is obtained by quantifying the acceleration and deceleration of the body. While single-plane accelerometers measure movement in the vertical plane, triaxial-plane accelerometers measure movement in the horizontal, mediolateral, and vertical planes. The gathered values are recorded and then downloaded to a computer for analysis and interpretation. The primary advantages of activity trackers are that they are small, lightweight, and usually noncumbersome. Moreover, physical activity data can be recorded over prolonged periods of time, ranging from several days to even weeks.

- **Heart-rate monitors.** There is considerable range in the overall capability (and cost) of different models of heart-rate monitors. While some devices simply display heart rate in real time, others record heart rate for prolonged periods of time. Furthermore, some models permit setting target heart-rate ranges and will alert the user when heart rate falls below or exceeds established lower or upper heart-rate limits.

- **Be comfortable with basic technology.** This is the place to start. Most people have not grown up with the type of technology that is used today. You need to dive right in and emerge yourself in the world of the students in regards to technology. Use iPads, explore websites and social media sites, play video games. It is important you see the world through the eyes of our students to understand where they are coming from. But, also embrace that your students might know more about something than you. How they love to show the teacher something! In fact, challenge your students to teach you new things as often as possible.

- **GoNoodle.** There are many software programs such as GoNoodle, which allows for competitive activities. With this program, you can have competitions within the classroom or have competitions with other classes too. It allows for moderate to vigorous activities like running, which can be done in the classroom. Students simply stand by their desks and can perform activities such as running in place, hurdling in place, stretching, and other exercises along with the GoNoodle videos, which even includes Olympic athletes from their respective events.

- **BattleSuit Runner.** Put on your headphones, select your workout time and music playlist (automatically integrates into the game), and begin walking, jogging, or running as the story and battles unfold based on your speed. You'll be prompted to slow down, speed up, and even sprint in order to effect the outcome of each mission. After each workout, use resources collected to upgrade your BattleSuit's capabilities for the next mission! BattleSuit Runner Fitness is a new, super-interactive story-running fitness app. It's part sci-fi adventure game, part GPS fitness trainer, part choose your own adventure—all for just a fraction of the cost of a single fitness class or session with a personal trainer (https://itunes.apple.com/us/app/battlesuit-runner-fitness/id775454936?mt=8)!

- **realindoor.com.** This site uses Google Street View to create a course for stationary bikes and treadmills, but can also be used in a classroom setting. Have the students jog in place beside their desk as they visit historical sites, faraway states, and exotic biomes. This is a great prelude to a lesson, while getting your students involved and "in the zone."

- **Allow students an opportunity to work with devices they are familiar with and which can enhance their development.** Our younger students work with Lego and on SCRATCH and Hopscotch. In science class we also use the Xbox Kinect, as discussed earlier in the chapter. Our students have also partnered with the older students (ages 13–15) for consultation on their Xbox Kinect programming game design.

- **Introduce students to real-world technology.** It is crucial students have a chance to explore not only software development in different environments, but also have a chance to work with a variety of devices on which that software runs. Students should get to explore creating programs that use a variety of input—such as body gestures, brain waves, or audio—so that the people working with them can include those with limited physical capabilities (such as the visually impaired, amputees) or with limited movement. Students should also have experience working with other output devices besides screens, such as robots (which are used in almost every industry).

Key Points to Remember

- Too much technology in classrooms can have a negative effect on achievement, especially if it's sedentary.

- Use activities with KinectEDucation or GoNoodle to get students moving in the classroom.

- Introduce students to real-world technology, like robotics.

- High-achieving countries use less technology in the classroom.

- Technology doesn't bridge the socio/eco gap, but can actually increase the gap.

- Incorporate technology with collecting data from activities and even caloric expenditure of food. Make it applicable to their life!

Classroom Management Concerns

"Active children are focused on the task, not off task."

Brad Johnson

Let's be honest. One of the major reasons that we like students seated in their desks working is that the environment is quiet and controlled. We worry that anything beyond the seated position may cause chaos. In reality, it is not the moving and activities that cause classroom disruption, but rather the lack of organization and preparation for a classroom that is more physically active. As educators, we have been trained that students need to sit and listen to learn, when in reality, nothing could be further from the truth.

This chapter will offer ideas and strategies to help you feel more comfortable about including movement, physical activity, and more team-building ideas into the classroom. This is not your typical "how to manage a class," but it is how to manage a class where children can learn the way they were created to learn, through active learning. And remember: once it becomes a routine, you will be glad you changed how your classroom functions because students will be more engaged, focused, and on task, not to mention their achievement will improve. Aren't these the things we desire in a well-run classroom? You will learn through this book that many off-task behaviors are a direct result of sedentary learning.

For example, if you were in a business meeting with a group of adults and you asked them to get up and move around, you would hear a lot of moaning and groaning. However, with children, ask them to go sit still and listen and you will hear a lot of moaning and groaning. Now imagine students who have to sit still most of the day, they will find a way to burn off excess energy, even if it's misbehaving. Interestingly, teachers sometimes aren't willing to step out of their comfort zone, yet we expect students to do this every day by sitting still in a desk. The other point with the movement is that there is such a variety that it doesn't need to be seen as purely fitness or athletic, but as you show throughout the book, music, team building, and even play can be an integral part of learning. So, don't be afraid to try new concepts, in fact we suggest levels of inclusion so that you find your initial comfort level, but hopefully from that point you will continue to increase activity level in your class for the benefit of your students.

Even with this new found knowledge, some teachers may be hesitant to change the learning culture of your room because you like the classroom quiet and controlled, but is learning really occurring in this environment? Students may be a little rowdy at first, because of the novelty of doing something different. However, once it becomes part of the routine, students will adjust to it as simply their new active learning environment. For example, when I taught middle-grades science, I rarely had my students sit in a desk. One of the reasons is that, as a student, I had an aversion to desks. I was an athlete and, at six feet tall, I didn't fit into the desk well in school. I remember that by high school and college I would seek out a table and chair or put a regular chair by my desk, so I didn't have to try and wedge myself in a desk. So, in my classes, I didn't care if students sat in their desks or not.

So, whether it is fear of chaos or you don't like you feel like some activities are out of your comfort, then start with activities in your comfort zone and then build the confidence to try even more activities in the classroom. Part of managing the classroom is your level of comfort with the activities and the ability to keep students engaged. For example, there are some teachers who really are into fitness and so doing many of the activities in the core and balance section would be a natural fit. But maybe you are hesitant to jump into those right away.

For example, you may only feel comfortable having students stand up or move around every 15 to 20 minutes. And guess what? This is still better for the students than not moving at all! In fact, as Dr. Benden shared from his research, "something as simple as stand up rather than sit, or have moving around in class actually increases caloric expenditure by 25–30 percent per day, which means improved weight control for students." He also added that this movement changes our metabolic profile by improving lipoprotein levels as well as blood glucose levels. That piece of data alone should make you want to change the structure of your classroom!

As a middle-grades science teacher, I would let students sit on the floor, lie on the floor, or stand up if needed, so they could focus on learning. Beyond that, I would often have my class outdoors. I would take my students to the stadium, or even out on a nature trail and have class. When students realized that having class outdoors was going to be part of our weekly routine if they behaved, they were more diligent about their behavior and monitoring others' behavior so they would get to go outside. It was part of our routine, but they were also aware that it was based upon an expectation of good behavior in class.

Even in the classroom, I would allow certain students to go to the back of the classroom and do pushups in class to burn off their excess energy, and then they would return to their seat or group and continue to work. Yes, the first few times this was a little disruptive to the class, but after a few times the students no longer paid attention; it had become part of the routine. The key to my success is that these activities weren't a novelty, but they were an integral and consistent part of the class. I remember at one parent/teacher conference I had a parent, who was a professional athlete, ask me how I was able to control his son when he had issues on other classes. I shared with him that I allowed the student to do situps, stand up, and move around when needed, and it made all the difference in the student's behavior. Sometimes we confuse a student with pent-up energy as a bad student. Let them move, and see how their behavior changes.

The first step is to streamline your rules for the class and incorporate ideas for movement. Simplicity is best, especially when it comes to younger students. I remember asking a child of a friend how he was enjoying 4th grade. He said that his teacher had too many rules. He said they are so hard to remember but so easy to break. Even though he was sincere, I couldn't help but laugh at his honesty. And it made me wonder: are your classroom rules so hard to remember, but so easy to break? K-8 students don't need dozens of rules; they need high expectations that are reinforced with a few rules and consistent consequences. High expectations are important, because students will live up to your lowest expectations. So make expectations the priority and spend the first weeks of school developing a rapport and relationships with your students so they will want to live up to your high expectations.

But, children being children, you will need a few rules in the class, but don't have so many that they are hard to keep. Simply choose three or four important rules and make them clear as possible. For example, "Be respectful to all" could be a rule for the class. To make this clear, you will have to give numerous examples of what this looks like to the students so they understand and can also understand the consequences with breaking the rule. So, even in the active classroom, you really don't need to worry about more rules or creating a lot of new or different rules to fit the new environment. Just make sure students understand the rules and the consequences for breaking them. Then make sure you consistently follow through with consequences. Otherwise, the rules are not worth the paper they are written on.

You should limit your rules, because you need to know them well and if a child stretches those rules even a tiny bit, call them on it. You can get a little more laid back as the year goes on, but make no exceptions for any class rules at the beginning of the school year. Not only do students have to learn your rules and expectations, they have to unlearn those of their previous teachers, because everyone has different rules or expectations.

The issue with some teachers is that they confuse rules and routines. But as Rebecca Alber (educational blogger for Edutopia) explains in her article "Back to School: Rules and Routines in the Classroom," rules have consequences and routines have reminders. Rules should be limited in number and have clear consequences. However, you will have more procedures and routines for the classroom. Some routines may only take several seconds to go over and then there are others that are more in-depth that take extra effort to explain and model. These may be the ones that require more movement, activity, or interaction in the classroom.

You will want to address all scenarios for starting class, getting out of one's seat, group work, or even going to the back of the class to do pushups. Keeping things consistent and controlled without too many rules in place is important. For example, a great way to start a class would be to have students do warm-up exercises by their desk while you play music. The students would quickly learn that when the music starts they need to stand up and exercise. One great warm-up is an exercise video by Dora the Explorer, where she performs several exercises to music.

There isn't really a limit to how many routines and procedures you have, but you will need to make sure that each one is clear to every learner in your room over the first few weeks of school. Probably the biggest mistake teachers make is jumping into academics the first few days of school rather than developing the team mentality and ensuring students know the rules and expectations of the class. I can always tell the difference between a teacher who took the time at the beginning of the year to establish the rules and routines and a teacher who simply jumped into the curriculum, because the latter will still be dealing with the same behavioral issues that she did the first week of school.

Remember: expectations, rules, and routines are all part of managing an effective classroom. But make sure all of these are established with movement in mind. A 2008 study found that children actually need to move to focus during a complicated mental task. The children in the study—especially those with attention-deficit/hyperactivity disorder (ADHD)—fidgeted more when a task required them to store and process information rather than just hold it. This is why students are often restless while doing math or reading, but not while watching a movie, explained **Dr. Mark Rapport**, the supervisor of the study and professor of psychology at the University of Central Florida in Orlando.

As we will discuss throughout the book, children with ADD and ADHD need opportunities to move when they have too much energy. So, think of the various options discussed in the physical classroom chapter with stand-up desks, stability ball chairs, and even stationary bikes where students can burn off energy without interrupting class. These simple ideas alone can become part of the class routine and help any student focus and stay task better. It will take weeks to get your students to where you want them to be, and you will have to continually reinforce their behavior throughout the school year.

One final thought on rules and routines is that every incident should be handled on a case-by-case basis, because each child and situation is different. However, there should be a common thread running throughout and all kids should see a clear connection between what they do and the resulting consequences. It's usually best when you can tie the consequence directly to the child's action whenever possible. And please don't think that taking away recess, silent lunch, or any of the typical consequences are effective. In fact, when I hear of teachers taking away recess or making students sit silent at lunch, first I want to scream, but I can guarantee them that they will continue to have issues with this student because they aren't focusing on solutions to the problem. They are just making the problem worse by taking away their outlets to release energy.

In the active classroom, students must be led to understand that when they follow the classroom expectations, they earn privileges and additional freedom, and you trust them with fun activities. Similarly, they must learn that when they don't contribute to an orderly classroom, you have no choice but to pull in the reins. This must be instilled at the beginning of the year, because students do not automatically make the connection between what they do and what you expect them to do. Finally, as we close the chapter on planning to move, keep these four ideas in mind:

1. **Planning.** Finally, create a weekly plan scheduling classroom activities. Indicate whether children will be working independently, in groups, or as a whole class. In a multi-grade classroom, each group may be working on a different activity.

2. **Connecting learners to activities.** Whether the learning activity is whole-class discussion or projects pursued by groups, you can introduce it by addressing the class in direct instruction. Try to make the information or skills to be learned meaningful to students.

3. **Connecting learners to each other.** Take advantage of the ways children can help each other learn in pairs and groups. One of the most important aspects of team-building and incorporating physical activities in the classroom is that certain students will be leaders depending upon the activities. This will give every student the chance to be successful and show their talents in the classroom. There is nothing more motivating than experiencing success.

4. **Guiding and observing.** When children are working independently on activities and projects (whether on their own, in pairs or in groups), move throughout the classroom, making yourself available for questions and guiding learners in overcoming obstacles. Use this time also for assessment, to determine how well children are focusing and the ways that they are interacting.

Ideas to Try

- **Start class with a mind warm-up.** I was trained to include a bell-ringer. This was an activity a student did when they came into the classroom for the first few minutes of class to get them focused. But if you want students focused, do some type of movement to get them focused. This can include one minute of music where they do certain movements like the Dora Explorer video mentioned above and in Chapter 8.

  Primary grades: Teach hand-clapping patterns to accompany a chanted verse or a set of math facts. Add foot-stomping or hand-clapping with a partner to create variety.

  Middle grades: Create a rhythm with finger-snapping and hand-clapping, which you model and they echo back. Vary the rhythm and pattern in intervals of 15–20 seconds to challenge them to pay attention and join in.

  Any grade: Offer a seventh-inning stretch, or the cross crawl. To do the cross crawl, stand up and begin marching in place, raising the knees really high. As you raise the left knee, reach across your body with your right hand and touch the left knee.

- **Play music to signal transitions to the students.** Children react to music in a way that they don't react to anything else. When a song comes on that they recognize and like, they'll notice right away. Use songs to welcome students to class, say "Hello," lead into circle-time activities, signal when it's time to clean up, practice ABCs, read a story, or other classroom activities. The students know exactly what to do when they hear the music and respond right away. Even when you don't play music as a cue, the students become so familiar with the language from the songs ("Clean up," "Make a circle," "Please sit down," etc.) that they will quickly follow the teacher's directions.

- **Play music to manage the energy level of the class.** You never know for sure what kind of energy level young children are going to come to class with. One day, you have a class full of children bouncing off the walls with energy (often on rainy days, when they can't go outside to play); the next day, the same kids seem like they are moving in slow motion. Music really helps to calm down a rowdy class, or give a lethargic class a needed boost of energy.

- **Play music to signal transitions to the teacher.** Plan your classes so that music accompanies the whole class. Use an iPod, or other MP3 device, to make playlists so that you don't need to change CDs during class. Before a 50-minute class, make a digital playlist of about 70 minutes' worth of music (50 minutes' worth of class-time music plus four or five songs to use as backups if you need to change activities or have extra time). If you don't have a digital music player, all of the Super Simple Songs CDs are designed to work great in a class, playing from start to finish. Each CD starts with a hello song, an active song, language theme songs, and then finishes with a goodbye song and a lullaby. You can just put the CD on and let it play.

  When you get to a section of the lesson where you need to concentrate on an activity, just turn the volume down and leave the music playing quietly in the background.

  When planning your lessons, think about how music can help you move from one activity to the next.

  Planning your classes with musical cues not only helps the students recognize what is happening next, but it helps you as a teacher move smoothly between activities.

- **Teach students how to collaborate before expecting success.** Doing project learning and other team-based work without prior training can lead to lots of dead time. You can nip much of it in the bud by teaching collaboration skills before projects get started. You don't need to use an activity related to your subject area to teach teamwork.

- **Allow students to move.** Allow them to shift in their seat, change seats, or move around every now and then. Provide quiet "fidget toys." This is crucial during times when you want him to take in a lot of info at once. The thing about attention deficit disorder is that it doubles a person's processing time. It comes across as the kids not paying attention, being disruptive, or rude. (We get very defensive when confused.) It does help, for whatever reason, to have something in the hands to fidget with, or even (I know this is an unpopular one) a piece of gum. By occupying the physical impulses, the brain works better and can concentrate.

- **Give the child important jobs to do**, especially ones in which he has to do something physical. "Joe, could you bring this to the office for me?" It is crucial that a kid with attention deficit disorder feels a part of things. Also, when confused, a lot of ADHD kids will get angry or violent. A prearranged signal between you and him could remind him that he is "floating out" and, if necessary, signal that he needs to take a short walk to the bathroom or water fountain to cool down.

- **Provide seating options.** As we discussed in Chapter 2, provide as much variety as possible for the students. Use stability ball chairs, stand-up desks, or even let students sit or lie on the floor. Remember: sitting at a desk is about the worst position to be in for extended periods of time.

Key Points to Remember

- *Baby steps.* Start at a level that you are comfortable with and, as you become empowered, include more activities in your classroom.

- *Routine.* When new activities become part of your daily plan the novelty will wear off and it will become routine for the students.

- *Music.* Use music to signal changes in activities or to begin/end class.

- *Beginning class.* Start class with an active movement to help students burn off excess energy. You will be surprised at how much easier it will be to manage behavior.

- *Flexibility.* Allow students to stand up, lie on floor, or even do exercise at the back of room if needed.

- *Limit rules.* Don't have but a few rules, but be consistent in monitoring them. Let expectations and routines be the main focus of managing the class.

Part III

Strategies to Try

Ways to Incorporate Movement in the Classroom

Activities to Reduce Stress

"It's not the load that breaks you down; it's the way that you carry it."
Lou Holtz (American football coach and analyst)

As we discussed in the technology section, children are exposed to more information by the age of 5 than their grandparents were by the age of 18. How many of you know it's hard enough as adults for us to try and digest and process all the stimuli and information that inundates us throughout the day? Can you imagine being a 6- to 14-year-old trying to make sense of all the "white noise" that deluges them on a daily basis? One study, by **Dr. Jean Twenge** (professor at San Diego State University and author of *Generation Me*), shows that five times as many students deal with stress, anxiety, and other mental issues compared to students during the Great Depression. Yes, five times more stressed than students who lived during the Great Depression! Can you even imagine?

The study found that, overall, an average of five times as many students in 2007 surpassed thresholds in one or more mental health categories, compared with those who did so in 1938. A few individual categories increased at an even greater rate—with six times as many scoring high in two areas:

- "hypomania," a measure of anxiety and unrealistic optimism (from 5 percent of students in 1938 to 31 percent in 2007); and
- depression (from 1 percent to 6 percent).

The study even suggests that the number may be even higher if so many students weren't already on medications for stress, anxiety, and other related issues. An increased emphasis on make-or-break school testing, and sharp focus as early as middle school on future college or career plans, can be intense for some kids. Other studies find that the ordinary struggles of adolescence—friendship, romance, fitting in—are magnified by social media that doesn't end when classes are over. In fact, stress has become a leading cause of sickness. Many doctor office visits are stress-related.

Our body is designed to deal with stress with a fight-or-flight responses, both of which are active responses. However, in schools, students aren't allowed an outlet for their stress. So they internalize it. High stakes testing, competition to get into colleges, grade-level promotion, and other factors, place more stress on students than in previous generations, yet we don't allow them to relieve the stress through active learning. Just as adults in the corporate world have learned to deal with stress through physical activities, focusing techniques, and other strategies, students need to learn these skills as well.

The absence of recess is also causing mental health problems among our younger students. When participating in daily recess, children learn to relieve stress and anxiety that is acquired throughout the school day.

The main cause of the students' stress is too much information crammed into their day. They are constantly being held to a high standard and often reminded of the pressure to succeed in areas like standardized tests. Many students feel overloaded constantly at school. One friend's child explained, "We have a lot of work all the time. It's a lot to do. I'm tired when I get home from school because even there I have more work to do."

Many people wonder why young students even have homework after spending eight hours a day in school. But, as we know, teachers often feel they have to send homework home because there simply isn't enough time in the day to get everything squeezed in. Teachers are constantly searching for time-efficient solutions, but it all comes down to one thing; everything's got to get done and there is just never enough time for everything to be covered in class.

The authors of "Robbing Elementary School Students of Their Childhood: The Perils of No Child Left Behind" believe that "physical activity does not reduce academic learning and it may actually increase it." Recess would allow the students to have time where they don't have to worry about grades or tests. Recess and PE also help our students' mental health by giving time for casual interaction with their peers. While in the classroom, students don't have much time to develop and contain healthy relationships with their peers, due to the enhanced curriculums and focus on testing.

Recess is a time where children play, laugh, and converse about things that do not involve schoolwork. It is a time for the brain to take a break from formal learning and engage in social learning. This is the time where the building blocks of relationships happen. This is a place where children learn how to socialize with others that are around them. It not only allows them to meet other students, but to make friends that are not in their classroom. Developing good people skills at an early age helps childhood with developing relationships throughout their life. Research studies have shown that children who actively take part in recess have better self-esteem, for it is a place for children to learn about their own abilities, perseverance, self-direction, responsibility, and self-acceptance. They begin to understand which behaviors result in approval or disapproval from their peers. So, even if your school doesn't have a formal recess time, take time breaks through the day (indoor or outdoor) to include this important part of education.

As **Dr. Marilyn Wedge** (author and therapist) explained in our interview:

Unstructured, non-goal-oriented play is essential for healthy psychological development as well as for fostering creative thinking in children. In play, the child creates a world into which she puts her thoughts, her imaginings and her feelings. The world she creates in free form is literally made out of herself, spun out of her own subjectivity. This created world, in turn, gives the child a sense of herself as an active, creative being. The child is the ruler of her tiny kingdom, and in it she feels deliciously free and alive.

The achievement-oriented, overscheduled, video game-intoxicated child of today misses out on the opportunity to create his own imaginary world. The absence of creative play and the growing emphasis on achievement narrowly defined is *stressful* to our children, because it frustrates and denies their need to build a sense of self through play.

There are also grave consequences for our society as well, for the loss of free play means a loss of creativity. Psychoanalyst and pediatrician Donald Winnicott says in his classic work *Playing and Reality* that the ability to play, to engage in the creative process is, more than anything else, what makes life worth living. Without it, a person becomes *depressed*. And, according to Winnicott, what allows an adult to engage in this meaningful process of creativity is the childhood experience of creative play, free from the rules and restraints of the adult world.

Part of dealing with stress is to understand how to cope with stress and handle failure. There is a lot of discussion, articles, and even books focused upon "Grit." This is simply a term that means "to preserve" or a "stick-to-it-iveness" where you don't give up. One example I always share about perseverance and attitude deals with athletes. In the Olympics, for instance, research suggests there is only a 3 percent gap in performance/ability between medal winners and athletes who barely missed making the Olympic team. A 3 percent gap means that their physical abilities are very closely matched. This also means that the ability to handle stress, and utilize coping skills, can be the difference between even making the team and winning a medal. The difference between winning a medal and not even making the team has very little to do with their physical abilities, but has everything to do with their attitude, coping skills, and mental state of mind.

Now consider how students stress out about performing on standardized tests. What if the difference between high-performing and low-performing students isn't about mental ability, but the ability to handle stress and utilize coping skills to perform better? Think about how many students are diagnosed with test anxiety. Why is this? What can we do to help them overcome the stress? Do we ever focus on bringing these strategies into the classroom to help improve students' academic performances? Even athletes who learn how to cope and use strategies when they are competing may not recognize that these same skills can be transferred into the classroom for academic performance. While these strategies will be discussed more in depth in the "Ideas to Try" section, some of the skills include anxiety reduction, positive self-talk, and goal-setting. Once students understand that they can overcome failure and setbacks, they are more confident and willing to take on more risks to be successful. It is about students learning to take control of their situations/environment and creating a positive outcome.

Finally, an important skill related to perseverance and coping is the ability to make good decisions. Decision-making is one area where students often have limited experience. Whether it is school, home, or extracurricular activities, students' days and activities are often set for them. There is not a lot of decision-making they have to do. This means that, when they are presented with a problem, they may not be equipped to make good decisions and therefore have to deal with negative consequences. But imagine if students were better equipped with better decision-making skills. Building skills like grit and perseverance will help increase college readiness.

Ideas to Try

I know you may be envisioning your class sitting around chanting to as a way to handle stress, but the following techniques are methods used by adults, athletes, and even in corporate settings to help employees perform more effectively. For some additional ideas, check out http://www.healthiersf.org/resources/pubs/stressRed/StressReductionActivities.pdf

- **Teach physical relaxation skills.** Another way to help kids in classroom settings where they cannot always move as they'd like is to show them how to modulate their physical tensions through specific relaxation techniques using yoga, progressive relaxation, isometrics, breathing, and imagery. See Armstrong's *ADD/ADHD Alternatives in the Classroom*. Here are some examples:

  - One of the simplest techniques is to teach a student how to alternatively flex and relax different muscles in his body to help discharge some of the muscular tension that he wants to express in more overt ways (this is called *progressive relaxation*). You can teach students a one-minute progressive relaxation procedure that they can do at their desks quietly without others in the classroom even noticing.

  - Similarly, you can show students how to take a deep breath, hold it briefly, relax, then repeat the procedure a few more times, as needed. Such deep breathing can help some students discharge physical energy and also center their focus of attention when they feel fidgety or restless.

  - Use visualization strategies involving kinesthetic imagery, such as letting students know that they can "physically move around in your mind" (e.g., "Do 40 push-ups in your imagination") instead of moving around the classroom. This can help students transform their physical energy into mental energy, which can then be "acted out" internally with no disruption to the class.

- **Refocus.** Provide students an opportunity during the day to refocus. Use a bell or xylophone and have students stop, breathe, and listen to the sound until it stops. This allows them to quietly reconnect to the present moment. It can be used to initiate discussion about the benefits of refocusing in the classroom. It can be used if students feel overwhelmed and need a break. This is a tool that can allow them to be able to persevere.

- **Teach self-talk.** What does perseverance sound like or feel like inside? It's often hard to recognize and even harder to develop without coaching. What phrases resonate for you? For your child? How about "I can make this work," "Don't give up," "I am blessed," or even "Challenges are made to overcome"? This helps students when they have failed in an activity to overcome the failure and look forward to the next task. It helps them realize something positive about themselves and gives them confidence to continue on.

- **Goal-setting.** The key here is to develop some attainable goals. Discuss the difference between short- and long-term goals. Give examples of each and then let students set and track their goal progress. Discuss when goals are not reached. What happens then? Do they fail and do they quit? Do they make different goals? Goal-setting helps students continue to progress and reevaluate often. This can help with experiencing success and failure and learning how to cope with each situation.

- **Challenge excellence in the classroom.** Real growth happens when people work at the edge of their competence. Students who are not challenged lose out on the sense of confidence that comes from mastering a challenge, and they may come to believe that accomplishment should be effortless. Challenging means that failure is possible. Bring students to that level. Let them fail. Allow students to rework certain assignments. This helps students understand that work can be improved and that mastery should be a goal when working as well.

- **Animal charades.** Students participate in a fun physical activity to reduce stress and tension. Students pick a paper from the hat and figure out how to present their animal charade. Since charades is a nonverbal activity, playing music in the background can add to the fun of "acting out" the animals.

  1. Depending on class size, break class into groups of two, three, or four students.

  2. Write several different names of animals on paper; one name per folded-up piece of paper (students may help with this as part of the activity).

  3. Put names in the hat.

4. Each group picks a name and figures out how to present their charade to the class.

5. Each group takes a turn presenting their charade, while the "audience" guesses the animals presented.

6. Depending on time, number of groups, and number of folded papers, teacher determines how many rounds of charades each group presents.

- **Deep breathing exercise** (belly breathing). Students practice deep breathing techniques as part of stress reduction. Teacher/facilitator introduces and demonstrates the concept of deep breathing as a stress reduction strategy that can be used in the present moment as well as an excellent skill to master to more effectively cope with future stressors. Teacher/facilitator has all students stand with comfortable space between each other or seated in a chair. Provide students with the following directions:

1. Stand straight up with feet shoulder-width apart.

2. Arms and hands are relaxed downward.

3. Body is relaxed.

4. Eyes are closed.

5. Focus on lower abdomen (belly) and imagine a small balloon in that space.

6. Breathe in slowly and deeply through nostrils, imagining the balloon inflating (getting bigger/larger/growing) slowly; hold a few seconds.

7. Slowly exhale through the mouth, imagining the balloon gently deflating (getting smaller, shrinking); blow out of the mouth as if blowing out a candle.

8. Tip: place a hand over the lower abdomen to feel it go up and down, and make sure you're not breathing with the chest.

9. Repeat at least 10 times. Ask students how different their bodies feel after the exercise. (Are they more relaxed/calm? Do they feel lighter? Great? Tired?)

Key Points to Remember

- Many social/coping skills are learned through play/recess.

- Teaching short-term and long-term goal-setting is important.

- Remember that attitude is everything! Having a positive attitude and working on skills to keep attitude optimal are critical for dealing with failure or overcoming obstacles.

- Provide strategies for dealing with stress and failing with the first few attempts.

- Help them with organization and planning skills.

- Positive self-talk. Redirect students' self-defeating language— focus on can, not cannot.

- Physical activity is a great stress reducer. Let students learn on their feet!

Activities to Help Students Focus

"I think the demand is so strong on sitting and learning, and for our multi-sensory learners, ADHD or not, they can't and won't learn by sitting and listening. Some educators are quick with the 'there's something wrong' theory when a child can't sit still. Some of us are more antsy than others. That's temperament, not ADHD."

Dr. Liz Matheis (clinical and school psychologist)

I (Brad) remember taking biology during my first year of college. I had a college professor who talked about ADD and ADHD even back in the 1990s. He said there wasn't a rise in ADHD, but that children simply didn't go outside and play like in the past. I think he may have been right, because as a child I spent a lot of time outdoors playing. If I had spent more time indoors, I am certain my mom would have thought I had ADHD as well.

Over the past several decades there has been a substantial rise in the diagnosis of ADD and ADHD. Over the past decade, ADHD diagnosis has risen approximately 25 percent. As **Allen Frances**, Professor Emeritus at Duke University, explains, "The rate of ADHD in the USA has tripled to 11 percent. One in five teenage boys is diagnosed and one in 10 is on medication. And the youngest kid in the class is almost twice as likely to be diagnosed as the oldest. We have turned immaturity into a disease." Regardless of whether or not you agree with him about how ADHD is overdiagnosed, these stats about the increased rates are powerful.

Many wonder why there has been such a significant rise in diagnosis. According to the CDC (Centers for Disease Control), two million more children in the United States have been diagnosed with attention deficit/ hyperactivity disorder (ADHD) and one million more U.S. children were taking medication for ADHD over an eight-year period (2003/4 to 2011/12). While we can't say with certainty whether or not there is an overdiagnosis of these issues, we can say that focusing only on medication is not the solution. But, there does seem to be a growing problem with medicating students for simply being overly energetic or, as we like to say, being kids.

This overmedication of students is what we refer to as the meducation of public schools. In 2010, the U.S. Centers for Disease Control and Prevention (CDC) claimed that one in 10 American children had ADHD, representing a 22 percent increase since 2003. Many of these kids are diagnosed based on highly subjective observations of parents, teachers, and guardians, and about two-thirds of those children were put on some form of prescription medication. Data from IMS Health found that 48.4 million prescriptions for ADHD stimulants were written in 2011, a 39 percent jump from 2007. And close to 14,000 new monthly prescriptions were written for ADHD stimulants, up from 5.6 million in 2007. It seems that, while medication use has skyrocketed, physical activity has plummeted during the same time period.

In 2013, researchers analyzed the results of 50 studies that included fitness results on more than 25 million kids from 28 countries. Overall they found kids to be less fit than their parents were, but the numbers were even worse in the USA. From 1970 to 2000, the results showed a 6 percent decrease in fitness levels per decade, which would now make it close to 20 percent. Medications on the rise, and fitness levels on the decline, and we don't see this as a public health issue with our students/children?

The good news is that we can reverse the trends. Recent research found that kids who took part in a regular physical activity program showed important enhancement of cognitive performance and brain function. The findings, according to University of Illinois professor **Charles Hillman** and colleagues, "demonstrate a causal effect of a physical program on executive control, and provide support for physical activity for improving childhood cognition and brain health." If it seems odd that this is something that still needs support, that's because it is odd, yes. Physical activity is clearly a high, high-yield investment for all kids, but especially those attentive or hyperactive. This brand of research is still published and written about as though it were a novel finding, in part because exercise programs for kids remain underfunded and underprioritized in many school curricula, even though exercise is clearly integral to maximizing the utility of time spent in class.

So, children are going to class with bodies that are less prepared to learn than ever before. With sensory systems not quite working right, they are asked to sit and pay attention. Children naturally start fidgeting in order to get the movement their body so desperately needs and is not getting enough of to "turn their brain on." What happens when the children start fidgeting? We ask them to sit still and pay attention; therefore, their brain goes back to "sleep."

Fidgeting is a *real* problem. It is a strong indicator that children are not getting enough movement throughout the day. In a 2009 study of preteen boys, University of Central Florida professor **Mark Rapport** found that the boys, especially those with ADHD, fidgeted more when a task required them to store and process information in their "working memory." Just as adults drink coffee to stay alert during a boring meeting, ADHD kids squirm and fidget to maintain alertness.

"Think of exercise as medication," says **John Ratey**, MD, an associate clinical professor of psychiatry at Harvard Medical School: "For a very small handful of people with attention deficit hyperactivity disorder (ADHD/ADD), it may actually be a replacement for stimulants, but, for most, it's complementary—something they should absolutely do, along with taking meds, to help increase attention and improve mood."

It appears that naturally occurring hormones and chemicals may be the best method for helping increase attention. During physical activity, endorphins are released in the brain. Endorphins are hormone-like compounds that regulate mood, pleasure, and pain. That same burst of activity also elevates the brain's dopamine, norepinephrine, and serotonin levels. These brain chemicals affect focus and attention, which are in short supply in those with ADHD. "When you increase dopamine levels, you increase the attention system's ability to be regular and consistent, which has many good effects," explains Ratey, like reducing the craving for new stimuli and increasing alertness.

As Dr. Mark Benden shared in our interview, "You can't operate the brain without the body operating at its peak, and our bodies are definitely not operating at their peak when they've been lethargic for a while. Your blood sugar is affected, and you get in a stupor. You think better on your feet than your seat!" Dr. Benden added that, in his research in pilot schools across Texas, there has been a decrease in medication dosages for ADHD students who are participants in their active classrooms. They have also seen a significant decrease in the BMI (body mass index) of overweight or obese children who are in these active classrooms as well. These statistics alone should have every teacher scrambling to make their classrooms more active. Imagine students reducing the amount of medication they have to take and students improving their fitness levels simply by being more active.

However, because of research from people like Dr. Benden, more schools are including exercise in their curricula to help kids do better in the classroom. A school in Colorado starts off students' days with 20 minutes of aerobic exercise to increase alertness. If they act up in class, they aren't given time-outs but time-ins—10 minutes of activity on a stationary bike or an elliptical trainer. "The result is that kids realize they can regulate their mood and attention through exercise," says Ratey. "That's empowering."

Finally, Dr. Spyridoula Vazou, a professor at Iowa State University, weighed in on the importance of exercise as it relates to learning and focus. She shared in our interview,

It is very important to focus on different types of exercise in order to improve students' focus and cognition. Recent research findings show that the benefits of exercise on cognition are not evident only due to the quantitative characteristics of aerobic exercise (such as the intensity and duration of running, biking, or walking), but also due to the qualitative characteristics of exercise (such as the focus on balance, coordination, and complex motor tasks) and the degree of cognitive engagement during the activities. Activities that offer these additional ingredients include yoga, martial arts, dance, as well as sports and motor skills such as dribbling, juggling, balancing, and gymnastic routines. A recent study by Dr. Caterina Pesce in Italy found that a PE program incorporating coordination and complex motor tasks was more beneficial than traditional PE in children with Developmental Coordination Disorder (DCD). Unfortunately, the number of studies that have examined different characteristics of exercise (as I described above) as well as different populations (e.g., ADHD, dyslexia, autism) is still small but the initial findings are very promising.

In general, research shows that children who are more off-task in class, as well as children with ADHD, are the ones who benefit the most from exercise, showing the largest improvements in concentration and self-control during instruction. Adding core, balance, and coordination activities in the classroom is very feasible (they do not require much space) and should be encouraged. We shouldn't only think of marching, running, and jumping in place as the only possible options for introducing movement in the classroom. Short dance routines requiring coordination, yoga, core exercises, juggling (even with paper balls), and balancing can also be practiced in the classroom. We also shouldn't forget that most of these examples include a high level of cognitive engagement, which is also very beneficial for students' focus, self-control, and learning.

A glowing example of how exercise in the classroom can help students with behavior problems, ADHD, and other issues is a school City Park Collegiate High School. This is a Canadian alternative high school in Saskatoon, Saskatchewan. **Alison Cameron** teaches 8th-grade students, almost all of whom have learning disabilities, behavioral problems, and domestic or personal issues. Approximately 50 percent of her students have ADHD. Class disruptions are commonplace in her classroom and most of her students are working at a 4th-grade level. Cameron did some research and found that students tend to behave better in class after doing physical exercise like going for a jog. So she got permission to purchase treadmills and bikes to place in the back of her class.

When she introduced the students to the fitness equipment and her new approach, the students weren't exactly thrilled with the thought of exercising. Some refused, but some joined her and would do about 20 minutes of cardio each morning. Gradually the rest of the students decided to try it, even if some could only go for five minutes initially. Since Cameron began her learning-with-fitness program, her students are focusing better and working harder, and they are less defiant. Students admit that they feel better about themselves and that it has helped them concentrate better in class. After only four months, Cameron's students improved a full grade level on average in reading, writing, and math. As Cameron shared in an interview with Phil Lawler (discussed in *Game Changer*),

> Everyone changed. Kids started getting off Ritalin. A student who could barely sit still for 10 to 15 minutes could sit quietly and complete an assignment for the first time. Students could concentrate and work harder. Not to mention an improvement in reading and writing of 25 to 30 percent. One student had a 400 percent increase in comprehension. Math performance was up 25 percent.

There should be no doubt in your mind that if you increase the physical activity of your students, you will see similar benefits, so what are you waiting for? Get your students learning on their feet!

Ideas to Try

- **Classroom warm-ups.** Establish a routine where you begin every class with activities in which you do something physical. Whether it's a quick classroom stretch, walking around the room, or even a few jumping jacks, this can be a great way to start the class off right or pump some energy into dozing students.

- **Take a hike.** Outdoor exercises like hiking are especially good for high-energy kids. Unlike with many team sports such as basketball, baseball, and soccer, there is no standing-around time. Your students will be constantly moving and using large muscle groups, keeping them focused. I taught middle-grades science for several years, and at least two times a week I would take my class for a nature walk for 15–20 minutes. Their focus and improved behavior was noticed by other teachers, as well.

- **Ode to movement.** Unlike other activities that work either the right or left side of the brain, music exercises both sides at the same time, training your mind to multitask better. If your kid is in a band, orchestra, or a choir, they are learning to work as part of a team—a key skill for kids with ADHD.

- **Pre-tech games.** Before you judge—isn't bingo for old folks?—remember that simple games are great for shorter attention spans, and small, frequent wins can build self-esteem. Eventually, your kid will gain the confidence they need to play longer, more strategic games. Games like bingo or checkers can be a great way to get kids to refocus.

- **Weeee. Or is that Wii?** There are many physical activities which can be incorporated into the classroom through videogames such as Wii, or online with sites like GoNoodle, which allow students to do activities like running in place against computer-generated opponents while standing next to their desks.

- **Classroom circuits.** Use a circuit of balance and core exercises that can be used in the classroom. These are exercises that specifically target the frontal lobe of the brain, which is the area of executive function. This benefits students with ADHD, dyslexia, and even autism. Examples are demonstrated in Chapters 9 and 10.

- **Light exercises.** Kids doing light physical exercises breathe normally as they do basic gross motor activities at a controlled pace. Below is a list of physical activities that can be done in the classroom at any time.

○ **Sky reaches.** Do this three times:

1. Stand up.
2. Swing arms up to the sky.
3. Rise up on your tippy-toes.
4. Reach for the sky while keeping your body tight.
5. Hold for 15 seconds.
6. Lower your heels and arms.

○ **Shoulder blasts.** Do these 10 times:

1. Hold your arms straight out to the sides.
2. Make arm circles forward (start with small circles, then gradually larger circles).
3. Reverse direction and make arm circles backward (large circles, then gradually smaller circles).
4. Raise your arms in front of your body and move your arms up and down.
5. Raise your arm above your head and wave them side to side, like a windshield wiper.
6. Pump your arms above head to "raise the roof."

○ **Squats.** Do this 10 times slowly:

1. Stand with your legs a little wider than shoulder-width apart.
2. Hold your arms out in front of your body.
3. Slowly bend your knees and squat down until your thighs are parallel to the floor.
4. Rise up slowly.

○ **Hand walks.** Do this five times:

1. Bend forward at your waist.
2. Reach down and touch hands to floor.
3. Walk your hands out for a count of 8.
4. Walk your hands to left for a count of 4.
5. Walk your hands back to the center for a count of 4.
6. Walk your hands right for a count of 4.

7. Walk your hands back to the center for a count of 4.

8. Walk your hands back for a count of 8.

○ **Star jumps.** Do this 10 times:

1. Squat until your thighs are parallel to the floor (see "Squats" above).

2. From this position, jump up reaching your hands and feet out like a star.

3. Land softly on your feet, dropping back to the squat position.

○ **Mountain climbers.** Do 20 foot switches:

1. On the floor, go to a plank position by putting your hands flat on the floor, hands shoulder-width apart, arms straight, and back flat.

2. Mimic a running motion by switching one foot at a time. Students can add intensity by adding speed.

Key Points to Remember

- Fidgeting students don't need to be still, they need to move!

- Physical activity, especially core exercises, can help students focus.

- Most children lack in core development and balance, which causes them to be off-task or disengaged.

- Exercise helps stimulate executive functions in the brain, which benefits students with ADHD, dyslexia, and even autism.

- Students learn better on their feet than their seat!

- Provide opportunities in the class for students to burn off excess energy.

- Children need frequent breaks!

Activities to Promote Teamwork

"Alone we can do so little: together we can do so much."

Helen Keller

When you think of the word "team," what comes to mind? Do you think of people sitting around leisurely? Or do you think of people in action, such as a sports team, or maybe even a SWAT team? The word "team" elicits thoughts of people running, jumping, hitting, catching, and other "action" verbs. One of the best ways to keep students moving is to have them participate in team-building activities. Team-building is not only a great way to get students moving, but creates opportunities for our students to experience that sense of confidence and fulfillment that comes from being a contributing part of something bigger than themselves.

Being human is by far not a solo experience. In every direction we look, we see people functioning in teams: family, work, recreation, church, and even government. It makes sense that if we recognize people also have a variety of imperfections, coupled with the fact that people need to be able to function as members of a variety of teams, more focus should be given to enhancing team-building skills. Effective teams have clearly defined roles where communication and cooperation among team members evenly distributes responsibilities.

The *team* members not only share expectations for accomplishing group tasks, but trust and support one another and respect one another's individual differences. Personal goal-setting is key for people to get outside their comfort zones and strengthen those areas that hold them back from success (being shy, aggressive, inattentive, apathetic, controlling, insecure). Kids love to be challenged, they love to have fun, and they love to move!

Team-building will not only get students up and moving, but it will also prepare them for the job market. Most human resource directors acknowledge they look to hire people who are willing to work on a team and who can provide evidence of successful teamworking opportunities they have experienced. This only strengthens the fact that we need to give students the opportunity to work in collaborative groups and promote teamwork within our schools. It is already being adopted within major corporations.

In fact, teamwork has become such an integral part of the business world that Fortune 500 companies will frequently visit collegiate sports teams to see the infrastructure of how a successful team works. For example, Dell and HCA and other companies will visit teams like The Vanderbilt Commodores, because they know that students who participate in sports tend to have great teamwork skills, which are highly valued in the workplace.

Many teachers do group activities, but developing activities where students work as a team is different than just placing students in a group. A group has characteristics such as: members are given their tasks or told what their job is in the group; members work independently and they often are not working towards the same goal; members may have a lot to contribute but are held back because they were given a specific task; and members may or may not participate in group decision-making, if it even exists.

We spoke with **Jamie Shankles**, founder and director of the adventure-based counseling program Niyélo. She explains, "A team has characteristics that are different from a group. This doesn't mean that groups are bad or that there isn't a place for group work, because groups are often utilized in the school setting. However, teams have traits that have more specific goals to achieve." According to Jamie, the following are characteristics of teamwork or team-building:

- Provides an opportunity for students to offer their skills and knowledge, and in turn are able to contribute to the group's success.
- Students work interdependently and work towards both personal and team goals. When students work as a team, they feel a sense of ownership because they commit themselves to goals they helped create.
- Students collaborate together and use their talent and experience to contribute to the success of the team's goals.
- Members participate equally in decision-making, but each member understands that the leader might need to make the final decision if there is no group consensus.

Team-building is important for problem-solving, engaging students, and getting them more active. Team-building also benefits students in other ways, as well. Robert Slavin, author of *Student Team Learning: A Practical Guide to Cooperative Learning* (Slavin, 1991) shows the following benefits of team-building and team learning. These include:

- Team learning has its greatest effects on student learning when groups are recognized or rewarded based on the individual learning of their group members.

- Team-learning classes achieved significantly higher test scores than the traditional classes. The difference between the more and less effective cooperative-learning classes was that the effective ones stressed group goals and individual accountability.

- Students involved in team-building are more likely to make friends in class: they like and trust other students more than students who are learning individually.

- Students have more self-esteem, a very important consideration with female and minority students.

As you can see, the benefits of team-building or team learning are quite impressive. Not only does it benefit students as it relates to movement, higher engagement, and less off-task behavior, but it also benefits them academically. This reinforces the concept of this book in general, which is that students need to move and be active to learn most effectively. It also reinforces the value of team-building and teamwork for success in the corporate world. Remember: companies are looking to hire people who work effectively in team settings, so shouldn't we be preparing students to work effectively in team settings?

The main point that you must drive home in every activity is that *everyone matters*. We need each other in order to be successful in life. These types of team-building activities help students learn how to work with people who are different than themselves, and helps prepare them for success in the workplace. Remember: you are not just a teacher, you are in essence a life coach preparing students for the real world.

Students must learn how to successfully lead, as well as how to follow. To have a successful team, the players need to know how to lead and how to follow.

Finally, remember that the first step in establishing a team is to know your students. The beginning of the year is an excellent time to begin to develop teamwork and cooperation skills with your students. Here are two suggested activities that can be used at any time:

Ideas to Try

Team-building is essential to success in the real world. Many corporations focus as much on being a team player as they do on you GPA. So try some of the different ideas below that were provided by team-building expert Jamie Shankles. She uses many of these activities in schools, as well as to develop team-building in executives at some of the top corporations in the country. And as she explained in our interview, "Kids love to be challenged, and they love to have fun. It will be important to discuss the reasons you are doing the activity with your group before you begin ... and then it will be important to save enough time following the activity to process with them what they can learn from having the experience." Below are a few ideas you can use to challenge your students to strengthen those weak areas:

1. **Group juggle.** Group students into circles of seven to nine. Each circle group gets a number of objects to pass (e.g., beanbags, hacky sacks, rubber chickens). One person starts off with an object and throws it to a person across from them. The object is thrown around to all players to establish a pattern; after everyone has caught and thrown it once, it should arrive back at the first person. Try and avoid throwing to the person right beside you.

   Once the pattern has been established and followed a few times, the first person can start to add more objects, one at a time. See how many objects you can keep going in your circle without any being dropped!

2. **Rock-paper-scissors (RPS) chain.** Everyone finds a partner to play RPS with. Introduce yourself to your partner and then play. The losing player joins the winner's team by forming a chain (go behind and place hands on shoulders). "Chains" of players now find other "chains" and the leaders play against each other. After the RPS decision, the losing chain joins the winning chain *after* they pass each other shaking hands (or high-fives) and introducing themselves. Keep going until only two chains remain, and host the Grand Championship (best out of three)!

3. **Communication game.** *Equipment needed*: one dry-erase marker, paper towel and dry-erase board for every team of two people. The

teacher will one dry-erase marker, paper towel and dry-erase board for every team of two people.

Objective: The students will learn how important communication is when working with another person.

1st challenge: Students will be sitting back to back. One student will have the image of shapes (such as three triangles and circles in the righthand corner of each triangle). The student with the dry-erase board and marker must listen to their partner and create the shape. It helps if you give everyone a different card, so, as they are listening to others and their partner, they will not be able to cheat. It also helps if you line them up in a straight line so no one can see anyone else's drawings. So, on a straight line, they have room between each other or are spaced in different parts of the classroom away from each other.

2nd challenge: You change positions with a new drawing. (Teacher will hand them out or have them numbered on the back, so they know to go to the next number.)

3rd challenge: You change positions and this time you face your partner and talk to them and try to get them to draw what is on your sheet of paper.

4th challenge: You change positions with a new drawing, where the person faces their partner to get them to draw what is on your new sheet of paper.

5th challenge: You cannot use words at all when trying to get your partner to draw the shapes with a new drawing.

6th challenge: You change sides and give the partner a chance to try to play this game with a new drawing. Remember: no words.

Come together after the challenges are completed and discuss the importance of communication and how others hear what you say differently.

Debrief questions: How did you feel as the challenge got harder? What could make your team stronger? Do you think getting to know each other would make you a better team? If so, why?

4. **Minefield with a twist.** *Equipment*: You will need to do this outside in order to have enough space, and you can use rulers, ropes from recess, balls, cones (you borrow from the gym), books, shoes etc. You will need activity cards, see Activity 2. You will need blindfolds—one for every pair of students.

Objective: To get your partner across the minefield without touching any other objects.

Starting the game: The person that is blindfolded will be spun around three times and will face the direction of the minefield. If they can be prevented from even seeing it, that would be best so that they don't know the lay of the field. The spinning offsets this and gets them a little disoriented. The teacher will have to set up the minefield ahead of time. The end of the minefield usually narrows to a path, and sometimes students must wait their turn to get through the objects defining the end of the course.

Activity 1: The student guides their person with their voice only through the minefield and, if they touch any other student, their guide, or an object, then they must start over. Reverse the roles and get them comfortable doing this as a follower and as a guide.

Activity 2: Create cards that get students moving or maybe even just make it more fun, and have the students try to get through each of them before hitting something or getting through the course.

○ You must do five pushups before you start the course.

○ You must pick up two paper clips and put them in shoe before you finish.

○ Your partner that is blindfolded must shout out "Does anyone want to dance?" at least two times going across the course.

○ You must do 10 jumping jacks before you finish the course.

It is important they read the card to the blindfolded person and then begin. They will trade places and cards every time. You can get through 10 cards in 30 minutes with one class.

5. **Stepping stones.** *Equipment*: one block of wood or piece of carpet per person large enough for someone to stand on, but challenging for two people to stand on.

Challenge: Your group must cross a raging river together without losing contact with the stepping stones provided.

Rules:

○ Stepping stones may not be thrown into the river nor thrown from person to person.

○ Physical contact must be maintained on the stepping stones at all times, or that stepping stone will be washed away by the river and not be allowed to be used unless the group chooses to start over.

○ Stepping stones can be stepped on, but not used as skis.

- If someone chooses not to stand on their own two feet, they must have a spotter.

- If anyone touches the river with any part of their body, the entire group must restart at the beginning.

6. **Magic carpet.** *Equipment:* one 10 ft × 10 ft tarp. *Challenge:* Your group has been selected by NASA to test-drive their latest invention—a magic carpet. Have everyone stand on the carpet (tarp) before continuing to read. Imagine that you are far, far away in space flying this carpet and suddenly get sucked into a black hole! When that happens, your carpet flips over, and you are falling fast, as the magic is now on the wrong side! Without stepping off or allowing any part of your foot to touch the ground, your group needs to be able to flip the carpet back over to its correct position.

    Rules:

    - If contact with the ground is made, you must restart.

    - Do not allow anyone to sit on shoulders.

7. **Building blind.** For building blind, students work in groups of three or more. One student is the leader and the others are an engineer or builders. The leader can see a simple structure (usually made of Lego or other building blocks), but the engineer and builders can't see it. The leader must explain to the engineers how to recreate the structure and which pieces to use. The engineer must then explain to the builders, but cannot touch the pieces, so good communication skills are important. This activity can be related to science, because of the engineering connection, but can be used simply for team-building skills.

8. **Interdisciplinary units where teams are required.** A great unit to use with students aged 10–11 is based on the Olympics. Students are randomly assigned a country in which they have made the Olympic team. Here are just a few challenges the students have completed as a team:

    - Design a team flag (art teacher helps with this) and carry the flag in both the opening and closing ceremonies.

    - Write and perform a national theme song or anthem (music teacher helps with this).

○ Design the Olympic uniform (drawing on paper or iPads).

○ Compete in various events (metric Olympics based on AIMS activities).

○ Compete in teacher-generated team-building events (PE teachers join with the subject area teachers and help run events in the gym or outside).

The team members receive medals (paper with string) that they wear when they place in an event. The medal count is recorded throughout the games, just like it is in the Olympics. The duration of the unit depends on the teaching schedules, but we have found a week to be ideal.

Key Points to Remember

● Learning to lead and to follow is important for students.

● Including team-building activities can help students who struggle with independent work.

● Incorporate activities that require movement. Teams are usually in action, not passive.

● Participating in team-building activities help students work toward group goals, while being individually accountable.

● Success in the real world demands the ability of students to work in teams.

● Focus on students using their strengths and talents to enhance teamwork.

Activities to Engage Through Music and Rhythm

"Music and movement are vital to the creative educational process. We enable the whole child to grow emotionally, creatively, socially and cognitively."

Ellen Church

As the research throughout the book supports, movement and physical activity is important for focus, achievement, and engagement. It is also important for maintaining a healthy bodyweight as well. Obesity is a critical issue in our culture, and the importance of physical activity among students has never been more important. One way to get students moving is through music. Music in many ways is the universal language. It connects cultures, generations, and even socioeconomic groups. But, with its rhythm and beat, music is a great way to help students move in the classroom.

I remember visiting Dr. Yvonne Sanders-Butler, principal of Browns Mill Elementary School, here in Georgia. I was interviewing her on the effects of childhood obesity. She had been overweight her whole life and had nearly died from issues stemming from obesity. She said that about eight years ago, as she walked through the cafeteria one morning, she noticed that many of her students were either overweight or obese.

She decided she had to make changes to her school. Yvonne said that before the changes, a large portion of the school would bring permission slips to skip PE and the kids didn't like to go outside and play. She knew PE wasn't working, so they changed the programs to involve more movement and dance that the children would enjoy.

She made several drastic changes, like reducing the number of processed foods in the school, and incorporating more movement into the classrooms. For example, she said they start every day with 10–15 minutes of music, and everyone in the school, even the administrators and staff, have to stop and move or dance to the music. By incorporating more activity into the day, especially with music, most of the students now enjoy PE and love going outside to play as much as possible. Yvonne said that standardized test scores have also improved significantly over the same eight-year period, so she knows it is effective.

The beauty of using music is that students don't need to be athletic or in great physical shape to move around. In fact, many of you may remember Richard Simmons, the fitness guru, who was obese as a child. He shared his story with me about how he didn't like PE in school because it was based upon competition. He said physical education back then consisted of playing sports like football and basketball. He said he was never picked to be on a team, so that made it even more of a turnoff. He had asthma, as well as knee and foot problems, so he didn't participate in PE very often.

While he didn't like physical education, running, or those types of activities, he realized that he did need to be active. So, he recalled putting his 45 rpm records on and dancing to them in his bedroom by himself. He didn't have to worry about competing with anyone or even if he had any rhythm—he just needed to move around to the music. Interestingly, Simmons took that same concept and created his own aerobics class using dance movements, and created some of the most successful aerobic videos of all time, such as *Sweatin' to the Oldies*. All of this success came from a student who didn't like physical education, and couldn't exercise in the traditional sense, but was able to lose weight through music and movement.

While listening to music is an auditory function, when movement is involved—such as clapping, dancing, and moving about—then it becomes a kinesthetic modality. That is why the previous stories are important to consider. Students cannot only enjoy music, and the effects of it on learning, but when movement is included it can also be beneficial to their overall health.

Music can also help focus a learner's attention. Music is sequenced, which helps us to recall memories. Information that travels on musical notes is learned more quickly and better retained for speedy retrieval. Think about how quickly a child can learn the lyrics to a new song they like. For the past 50 years, most children have grown up watching *Sesame Street* or reading Dr. Seuss. These use a lot of rhythm, sequencing, and rhyme to make children remember and make it fun.

In a study to examine the impact of music and movement on academics, **Janet Evans** (professor at Wayne State University) examined achievement in math of kindergarten students. According to her findings, music is an important part of a young child's growth and development. Music can also positively affect the quality of all children's lives. Through creative expression in rhythmic movement and listening experiences, music can help children emotionally and intellectually. Musical experiences should be a daily routine for all children. These experiences should be planned for different types of learning opportunities and with other subjects.

She states that, according to her research,

Math and science tend to be stronger in students who have music or an arts background. Spatial-temporal reasoning skills are crucial in learning certain math concepts. The value of music to spatial reasoning, creativity and other mathematical skills has long been established. Music strengthens the spatial-reasoning essential to math skills. Key math areas of the brain overlap with areas highly involved with music.

Research suggests that music often leads to the higher brain function typical of math. Music has a rhythmic quality to it that makes it easy to remember. Music not only supports the development of math skills, but many others too.

Research proves that music and movement are vital components in developing and enhancing student's performance in the area of math. If music can set the stage for learning, increase a child's interest, and activate a student's thinking, what are we waiting for? Music makes you want to move. Even if you have no rhythm, if you like the music you will begin to tap your feet or move in some manner. Allowing children to move freely to the music helps them learn about balance, coordination, motion, and much more. This type of creative movement is about more than just physical exercise. It is a connection of the brain, body, soul, and senses. Talk about teaching to the whole child!

Teachers can ensure that music activities are not being taken away from "academic" time by remembering that:

1. Musical activities are another type of instructional approach, like manipulatives and worksheets.
2. Music activities need to be used to specifically teach curriculum content that the students learn.

3. Music can be used to provide an introduction to stimulate interest in different subjects: "As one's base of prior knowledge grows, interest and learning becomes easier and a positive cycle is established."

One of the most innovative ways to include music in the classroom is to bring pop culture into the classroom. This is exactly what 2nd-grade teacher Carrie Swedicki did for her class. She weighed over 200 pounds when she walked by an arcade and saw the Dance Dance Revolution game. She decided to give it a try. She didn't do well her first time, and someone actually yelled "You suck" at her first failed attempt. But, she said those words challenged her to get better at the game. Over the course of a few years, she lost 75 pounds and decided to bring the dance revolution into her own classroom. She is now an advocate for using Dance Dance Revolution in the school systems as a tool to fight childhood obesity. She currently uses Dance Dance Revolution in her classroom for physical activity, not to mention fun!

While music can be energizing, fun, and engaging, it can also be a great source of focus, stress reduction, and even relaxation for students. Interestingly, stress is often reduced by movement itself. And students have stress! Think about the pressure we place on students, especially to meet certain standards on an exam so they can be promoted to the next grade. Yet we do very little in schools to help alleviate stress.

Another aspect of music, regarding stress relief and relaxation, is to play music that is soothing and can help lower resting pulse rate. Baroque (classical) music can be very calming in the classroom setting. When I taught science class, I would often play classical music when the students were studying for an exam, or reading text. The students enjoyed listening to the music and it had a very calming effect on all of them.

According to Emily Gunter (author of *Super Learning*),

It is a known fact that some music can be used to relax you. Conscious breathing to 60 beats per minute music, such as Baroque, helps to keep you in your relaxed system for Super Learning. The 60 beats per minute are important, because that is the rate your heart beats when relaxed. The music helps to remind you to breathe and stay relaxed. When you are studying with music in the background and you hear the music, this is a reminder to breathe deeply. While you are in the relaxed system you don't hear the music really. The music helps to create a peaceful relaxed environment, prime for learning and using long term memory.

Ideas to Try

● **Movement to music freeze dance.** *Target*: Activity is most appropriate for elementary students.

   Purpose: Gross motor activities provide stress reduction for young students.

Materials:

   ○ A CD, iPod (with portable speakers), or tape player.

   ○ Music (5 to15 minutes of music).

   ○ Note: It is best to use instrumental music/no lyrics; you may download music from an internet source (ask your music teacher).

   Content: Students move/dance to match the tempo, beat, and rhythm of the music. When the music stops, students *freeze*; when music resumes, students continue to move/dance to match the music. It is suggested that the sequence of music starts slow and calm, moves to fast, upbeat pace and then returns to slow and calm to end the activity.

Instructions:

1. If necessary, arrange classroom to provide ample space for the activity.

2. Students take a place in the designated "movement/dance" area with sufficient personal space so as not to run into other students, *or* students may be positioned in a circle and move in the same direction around the circle.

3. Review activity rules with students:

   ○ Move to match the music.

   ○ Freeze when the music stops.

   ○ When the music starts again, move to match the music.

   ○ Activity involves only movement, no voices.

4. Start the music.

5. Stop music at timely intervals.

6. Note suggested sequence of music; always end with slow, calming music.

   Extension: Teacher may follow up by using movement to match music at other times, to relieve tension and stress in the classroom. Make connection for students between regular physical activity, health, and stress reduction.

- **Play music to introduce new language.** Songs are a great way to teach new language to youngsters. Even when children don't fully understand all the lyrics, they are excited to try to sing along. When you have songs with simple lyrics that kids can dance and do gestures to, the children sing and learn more quickly.

- **Active learning experiences.** Music will activate students mentally, physically, and emotionally and create learning states which enhance understanding of learning material. As Chris Brewer suggests in his book *Music and Learning*, learn to activate information physically, play upbeat music during a related movement activity or role-play. For example, while learning about the flow of electrons in electricity, play Ray Lynch's *Celestial Soda Pop* while you create a classroom flow of electricity. Some students are stationary neutrons and protons, while others are moving electrons. When we add "free electrons," like a battery would, the electrons begin flowing and voilà! We have an electrical current! Ray Lynch's upbeat music keeps us moving and makes the role play more fun.

- **Creativity and reflection.** While the focus of our book is on getting students active and moving, there are times when they need to sit, reflect, and write. Background music is used to stimulate internal processing, to facilitate creativity, and encourage personal reflection. Research suggests that when music is played in the background, students are writing or journaling for longer periods of time than without the music.

- **History album.** Allow students to design a record album for an event or time in history. They should develop an album cover, complete with visuals on the front and a song list on the back. Students can create songs that relate to the place, time period, or event. They can also teach dances to accompany the songs, to incorporate more movement.

- **Multiplication song.** Learning the times tables can be tricky these days, since many kids need to be actively engaged in order to learn. We are always looking for innovative and unique methods to help students with multiplication, since these key facts set the foundation for advanced mathematics later on as children enter middle school and high school. Songs and rhymes are an age-old tradition which works especially well, especially for auditory learners. Songs for multiplication, skip counting, and even division can be found at www.songsforteaching.com/math/multiplicationsongs.htm

- **Class management.** I know teachers who use music to manage movement and transitions in their classroom. The way it works is that, instead of providing a verbal signal to initiate a routine, you would simply turn on a piece of music. Simply click a link on your iTunes or radio, and like magic your students would launch into action, putting away their work or lining up for lunch. There is some planning involved in selecting the right music to match a routine, and you'll want to practice with your class before putting it in play, but once they've got it, they've got it. When using this strategy for the first time, it's a good idea to start small. Choose a simple routine, like lining up to leave the room, and match it with a 60-second song.

- **To start school.** The moment the bell rings to start school, the lights go off, the music starts, and the day gets rolling. We play a theme song to start our day much as a theme song starts your favorite television show. This is usually an upbeat tune, and it's accompanied by some simple motions to get the students moving around and giving high-fives to their peers. It is a good wake-up call.

- **During transitions.** I have 10-second, 30-second, and one-minute sound clips. After the first few weeks, the students know exactly how long they have for a "Turn and Talk" or to transition to the next subject. Once they are used to the songs, you will see the talking in the room stop as the end of the song approaches.

- **Setting the tone.** Play upbeat songs to energize the class or during "brain breaks" or playtime. Play classical music to calm them down and to help redirect or focus them.

- **Scavenger hunt.** A great way to get to know what your students like is to do a scavenger hunt. It will ask questions like "What is your favorite type or music, favorite song, and favorite instrument?" or "What songs do you like to sing? What instrument do you wish you could play?" So, the students answer the questions, then they have to meet two or three new people in class and ask them the same questions. This is a great way for students to connect, but also to find out what music you can select to play in class.

- **Musical masterpiece.** This is a fun and creative way to get your students moving, especially elementary-age students. Each student begins drawing a picture on their desk, but when the music stops they move to another desk and continue to add to the next drawing. This continues until the teacher calls time. Then the students will use three or four colored pencil crayons and continue moving with the music, but now they will be coloring in the masterpieces.

- **Make your own music—elementary.** Most children are intrigued by songs that involve counting, spelling, or remembering a sequence of events. Songs and musical activities with other school subjects also are effective during this child developmental stage. So, create your own songs with students based upon content area, and don't forget to let them move!

- **Make your own music—middle.** Teenagers may use musical experiences to form friendships, and to set themselves apart from parents and younger kids. This can be part of subject content, or maybe be part of a creative writing assignment. One fun example would be to let them write songs for historical or fictional characters. For instance, wouldn't we all be interested in hearing a song that Romeo may have sung to Juliet?

Key Points to Remember

- *Mental capacity and intellect.* There is a connection between music and the development of academic thinking.

- *Mastery of the physical self.* Children develop coordination, which aids muscular development. They begin to understand what they can do with their bodies as they run, balance, stretch, crawl, and skip, especially to music.

- *Development of the affective aspect.* Through music and movement, children learn acceptable outlets to express feelings and relieve tension.

- *Development of creativity.* Such as creating songs and dance movement to music.

- Music can be used to reduce stress and calm students.

- Music can be used to manage movement, start class, end class, etc.

- Music is a great way to move and burn off energy!

9

Activities to Build Core Strength

"A strong core helps build the foundation for a strong mind."

Melody Jones

How often have you been teaching a great lesson, especially at the end of the day, to observe your students slumped in their desks, tilting back in their chairs, or even tapping a pencil on their desk? And how would you feel if your principal walked by and saw the students disengaged? You would probably be frustrated, but is this because you didn't have a great lesson or couldn't capture the attention of your students? Or is there another issue totally unrelated to your lesson?

Whether it is in the classroom or at home, children simply spend too much time sitting. It is rare to find children rolling down hills, climbing trees, and spinning in circles just for fun. Merry-go-rounds and teeter-totters are a thing of the past. Recess times have shortened due to increasing educational demands, and children rarely play outdoors due to parental fears, liability issues, and the hectic schedules of modern-day society. Let's face it: children are not nearly moving enough, and it is really starting to become a problem.

Angela Hanscom (pediatric occupational therapist) shared in an interview with the *Washington Post* how she did an observation of a 5th-grade classroom as a favor to a teacher. She said, "I quietly went in and took a seat towards the back of the classroom. The teacher was reading a book to the children and it was towards the end of the day. I've never seen anything like it. Kids were tilting their chairs back at extreme angles, others were rocking their bodies and forth, a few were chewing on the ends of their pencils, and one child was hitting a water bottle against her forehead."

This was not a special needs classroom, but a regular classroom. She thought the children might be fidgeting because it was the end of the day and they were simply tired. Even though this may have been part of the problem, she realized there was certainly another underlying reason.

After further testing, she learned that most of the children in the classroom had poor core strength and balance. In fact, they tested a few other classrooms and found that, when compared to children from the early 1980s, only one out of 12 children had normal strength and balance. Only one! Interestingly, the 1980s is when many schools began to reduce recess and playtime in schools. It is also when the rise in obesity began in the children at an alarming rate.

Many children, including children who participate in athletics, have underdeveloped cores due to restricted movement. In order to develop a strong core system, children need to move their body in all directions, for hours at a time. Just like with exercising, they need to do this more than just once a week in order to reap the benefits. Therefore, practicing for a sport or physical activity once or twice a week is likely not enough movement for the child to develop a strong core system.

Finally, Angela believes, "Children are going to class with bodies that are less prepared to learn than ever before. With sensory systems not quite working right, they are asked to sit and pay attention. Children naturally start fidgeting in order to get the movement their body so desperately needs and is not getting enough of to "turn their brain on." What happens when the children start fidgeting? We ask them to sit still and pay attention; therefore, their brain goes back to "sleep."

So exactly what are our core muscles? Most of us think about having that flat stomach or those great six-pack abs. The truth is, having a great strong core goes beyond having a nice looking midsection. The core is actually made up of multiple muscles that move, support and stabilize the spine. There are five different components of core stability: strength, endurance, flexibility, motor control, and function. It is important first to achieve the core stability to protect the spine and surrounding musculature from injury in static and then dynamic movements. This is a vital function in children who are athletic. Research has shown that athletes with higher core stability have lower risk of overall injury. The core muscles are responsible for your posture.

Your extremities and head all rely on your core for support and balance. Some of your back muscles are also considered part of the core muscle group. The strong back core muscles even support your abs and help assist you with actions such as sitting up at a desk, bending to tie your shoe or reaching up to take something off a shelf. Pretty cool, huh? Most of us don't actually realize how important having a strong core can play such an important role in the movements of everyday life. Having a weak core can definitely lead to bad posture, especially when sitting for hours at a time. This can really affect children when having to sit for long periods of time in the classroom. Because students sit for most of the day, they are eventually seen hunched over writing or staring at a computer screen. Some examples of student behavior with weak cores can include laying head on desk, leaning back in chairs, and lack of engagement, all of which have nothing to do with teacher or content.

While we discuss ADD and ADHD more in depth in Chapter 6, it is important to understand that the exercises in this section help develop the area of the brain where executive control occurs. "We've found exercise has broad benefits on cognition, particularly *executive functioning*, including improvements in attention, working memory and the ability to multitask," said researcher Charles Hillman, a professor of Kinesiology and Community Health at the University of Illinois at Urbana-Champaign. In fact, an active lifestyle during childhood may confer protective effects on brain health across the life span, Hillman said.

Executive function helps with focus, planning, organizing, and other skills that students have difficulty with who are diagnosed with ADD and ADHD. And when one in 12 students lack the core strength of students in the 1980s, it is easy to see why many students may exhibit some ADD traits or off-task behaviors, when all they need are stronger core muscles. As we mentioned in the introduction, all of these exercises and activities aren't as much about being physically fit as they are about improving mental focus, processing, and student achievement.

Finally, **Dr. Spyridoula Vazou** (assistant professor of Exercise Psychology and Pedagogy in the Department of Kinesiology at Iowa State University) shared with us that

> It is very important to focus on different types of exercise in order to improve students' focus and cognition. Recent research findings show that the benefits of exercise on cognition are not evident only due to the quantitative characteristics of aerobic exercise (such as the intensity and duration of running, biking, or walking), but also due to the qualitative characteristics of exercise (such as the focus on core, balance, coordination, and complex motor tasks) and the degree of cognitive engagement during the activities. Activities that offer these additional ingredients include yoga, martial arts, dance, as well as sports and motor skills such as dribbling, juggling, balancing, and gymnastic routines.

Ideas to Try

These exercises are important for developing the core muscles. Developing the core, as we have mentioned, also helps develop the frontal lobe of the brain where executive functions occur. The beauty of these types of exercises is that, even if children don't enjoy the competitive sports of physical education or running laps around a track, they will find these exercises more accommodating, even if they are challenging.

- **Plank.** Planking is one of the best exercises for a strong, tight core. This exercise activates all the core muscles by contracting at once. There are many variations of this exercise.

- **Side planks**
  1. Lie on side.
  2. Place forearm on floor under shoulder perpendicular to body.
  3. Place upper leg directly on top of lower leg and straighten knees and hips.
  4. Raise body upward by straightening waist so body is ridged.
  5. Hold position while contracting the core.

- **Wall sit**

1. Start with your back against the wall with your feet shoulder width and about 2 feet from the wall.

2. Slowly slide your back down the wall until your thighs are parallel to the ground.

3. Adjust your feet so that your knees are directly above your ankles (rather than over your toes).

4. Keep your back flat against the wall.

5. Hold position while contracting the core.

Note: You will also feel this in the lower body.

- **Superman/Superwoman**

1. Lie in prone position with arms and legs together stretched out.

2. Slowly raise arms and legs up in a holding position.

3. Hold position for desired length of time.

- **Single raised leg crunch using medicine ball or small object**

1. Start by lying on back.

2. Bend one knee while keeping opposite leg straight.

3. Slowly raise straight leg

4. Using your abdominal muscles, lift your leg up high the same time you crunch, using ball or object to touch your shin.

5. Lower your arms and leg back down to the starting position and repeat.

V-up

1. Start by lying on back with hands on floor over the head.

2. Raise straight legs and torso.

3. Reach toward raised feet and contract the core.

4. Hold for desired length of time.

- **V-up on BOSU®**

1. Sit down on BOSU® and slide down to center your body toward the middle of the BOSU®.

2. Slowly raise both legs in the air.

3. Raise upper body with both arms straight and in full extension trying to touch legs.

4. Contract core and hold for desired length of time while maintaining balance.

Adaptation: This exercise can be done on carpeting without BOSU®.

Key Points to Remember

- Most students have weak or underdeveloped cores.

- Simple exercises, even without equipment, can be incorporated into the classroom.

- Disengaged or fidgeting students may not be bored, but fatigued.

- Children should be up moving, not sitting for extended periods of time.

- Exercises can be done as whole class, or based upon individual need, during the course of a class or the day.

Activities to Improve Balance

"A coordinated body not only helps in injury prevention, but can improve kinesthetic awareness and mental processing."

Brad Johnson

The elementary years are not only an optimal time for children to learn through physical activity, but are also a critical developmental period. If children are not given enough natural movement and physical activity, they start their academic careers with a disadvantage. They are more likely to be clumsy, have difficulty paying attention, trouble controlling their emotions, utilize poor problem-solving methods, and demonstrate difficulties with social interactions. Pediatric therapists are consistently seeing sensory, motor, and cognitive issues arising in later childhood, partly because of inadequate opportunities to move, play, and be physically active.

For instance, by the time I was 4 or 5 years old, I basically lived on a bicycle. But many children today, including my nephews, never even learned to ride a bike. They miss out on developing many balance and coordination skills that we took for granted growing up.

So, what do balance and coordination mean for the classroom? *Balance* is when the body is in equilibrium and stationary, meaning no linear or angular movement. This is important, because balance is dependent on both the internal and external factors to maintain the body's center of gravity over its base of support. As we age, we tend to lose our ability to balance. This can also be seen in individuals at an early age. Even children can struggle with their ability to balance. This can be due to many reasons, such as being physically unfit, past and existing injuries, neurological, and mental issues.

Balance training programs are created to help prevent lower extremity injuries by improving balance ability in many types of individuals including those who are healthy and physically active.

As a trainer, I (Melody) notice that many school exercise programs focus very little on increasing balancing abilities. Balancing activities can be simple but challenging exercises that gain major benefits. According to *NASM Essentials of Personal Fitness Training*, balance training programs that are performed for at least 10 minutes a day, three times a week for four weeks appear to improve both static and dynamic balance ability. Therefore, having effective balance ability is necessary for both the healthy and the injured population. So, by training in a multisensory environment, this will increase the demand on the nervous system's ability to activate the right muscles at the right time in the right plane of motion. Balance and neuromuscular efficiency are improved through repetitive exposure to a variety of multisensory conditions. For example, stand with two feet on the floor, now try standing on one foot and try to balance for 20 seconds. Now you've taken a very simple exercise to another level. Not only is this type of exercise highly beneficial but, let's face it, kids love doing the activities and overall enjoy the challenge. So why not incorporate these activities into the classroom daily? Kids would actually look forward to doing these exercises and stay motivated when doing schoolwork.

As we discuss throughout the book, physical activity is beneficial for the brain and learning. However, as we also have shown, children today simply aren't as fit or don't have the strength and balance as children did in the 1980s. Interestingly, improving balance and coordination is not only important for being healthy and increasing neuromuscular efficiency, but also for improving some of the fundamentals of learning, like reading. In one case study (see http://integratedlistening.com/case-studies/dyslexia-adhd-apd/ for complete information), a 5th-grader was diagnosed with mild dyslexia, ADHD, and an auditory processing disorder. He was struggling greatly in the 5th grade with all subjects due to an inability to read fluently and difficulty with focusing. After initial evaluation, the therapeutic goals prescribed included improving coordination, balance, and core strength.

Upon re-evaluation, the student had made improvements in all areas noted initially as deficits. He demonstrated age-appropriate balance, coordination, strength, handwriting, body awareness, visual motor integration skills, and attention abilities. His mom reported improvement in handwriting skills, attention to tasks, and independence in completing tasks at home. She also reported decreased impulsivity with task completion and increased attention and self-confidence when attempting new tasks.

Researchers now know that students who have difficulty reading (reading words from left to right), such as the 5th-grader in the case study, tend to have balance issues related to movement across the midline of the body. This is important to understand, because it's not about the intellect of the student or how much time they spend studying, but rather it is a physical issue that affects their mental processing. Occupational therapy activities treat such problems with specific brain/body exercises, and we as classroom teachers can help, too, using activities that have children crossing the midline. One of the activities they recommend for movement across the midline of the body is *skipping*—yes, skipping! No wonder I can read and write so well! Other activities and games that they recommend are included in the Ideas to Try section for this chapter.

As we have discussed in other chapters, physically active children tend to perform better on tests than their sedentary counterparts. While part of it may be the increased fitness levels, oxygen intake, etc., there is also the coordination and balance competence that is often forgotten. But, as the research shows, students who increase their balance and coordination can and do show improvement in achievement. In fact, about 8 percent of students tend to have difficulties with coordination and with learning new skills, which affects their function and participation at home, school, and in the playground. These types of development coordination disorders are commonly referred to as dyspraxia. Developmental difficulties such as anxiety disorder, attention difficulties, developmental language disorder, poor working memory, and autism are all associated with dyspraxia. A lack of control and motor skills causes tasks such as reading, cutting with scissors, and even pouring water from a beaker to be difficult for these students.

In his book *Beating Dyspraxia with a Hop, Skip, and a Jump*, Geoff Platt explains,

> Children with dyspraxia often have reduced motor skills including balance, timing and coordination. It is no wonder then, that they will do everything in their power to avoid gym class! By encouraging children with dyspraxia to take part in an easy and fun exercise program, teachers and parents can help them to overcome their symptoms and enjoy physical activities.

I (Melody) remember working with a school in the Atlanta area recently on balance and coordination. The teacher thought the activities would be simple for some of the students because they played multiple sports and were very athletic. However, as we progressed through a sequence of balance and coordination activities, the teacher was amazed that the students lacked coordination and balance. What immediately became clear was that the students enjoyed the activities even if they didn't do them well. Apparently, since none of them were experts, they all enjoyed trying to improve together and the challenge was very enticing to them. Children loved to be challenged! Since they were all smiling, laughing, and begging to try more activities, it was apparent they all really enjoyed the activities. Imagine students enjoying learning and wanting to learn more!

However, if you recall from Chapter 9, only one in 12 children have the core strength and coordination of students from the 1980s, so it wasn't that surprising to me. Fortunately, there are many simple balance and coordination activities that can help all students improve their balance and coordination. These activities can be incorporated into the class as needed and can become a staple of recess and physical education classes.

Ideas to Try

Balance training is important, as it can improve postural alignment of the body and develop coordinated movement. Having good balance is an important skill to have when doing any type of day-to-day physical activity. As we age, we also lose the ability to balance, which increases risk of injuries. Having good balance skills will reduce chances of injury and increase dynamic coordination.

- **Hula hoop.** Hoops are able to spin around your body from the momentum you provide by rocking back and forth pushing your hip and belly forward, slightly shifting your weight as it spins around your waist. Every time the hoop hits your stomach, pushing your belly forward keeps the hoop in motion. Hula hooping helps strengthen core, but is also great for developing balance and coordination.
- **Standing balance on BOSU**
    1. Place one foot on the side of the BOSU and shift the ball to the side until it touches the floor. Do not remove your foot from the ball.

2. Now you are ready to step up with the other foot.

3. Make sure both feet are hip width apart and with toes pointed forward.

4. Stand upright on ball and slightly rock back and forth to get familiar with standing balance.

● Single leg balance on BOSU

1. Place one foot on the side of the BOSU and shift the ball to the side until it touches the floor. Do not remove your foot from the ball.

2. Now you are ready to step up with the other foot.

3. Slowly shift one foot toward the middle of ball until foot is directly in the middle.

4. Slowly bend opposite knee to lift foot up until you come to a complete single leg balance. Foot should point forward.

Adaptation: single leg balance can be done on floor, such as standing by desk.

- **Single-leg throw and catch**

    1. Stand holding a medicine ball with feet shoulder-width apart and pointing straight ahead.

    2. Lift one leg while maintaining optimal alignment.

    3. Gently toss the medicine ball to a partner, so they can catch it without stepping.

- **Single leg balance with medicine ball**

    1. Stand holding a medicine ball with feet shoulder-width apart and pointing straight ahead.

    2. Lift one leg while maintaining optimal alignment.

    3. Continue to hold medicine ball while balancing.

Adaptation: this exercise can be done standing on exercise mat or floor.

- **Single-leg lift and chop**

1. Stand holding a medicine ball with feet shoulders-width apart and pointing straight ahead.

2. Lift one leg while maintaining optimal alignment.

3. Lift medicine ball in a diagonal pattern until medicine ball is overhead as shown.

4. Slowly return to original position and repeat.

● **Planking on BOSU**

1. Lie prone on the floor with feet together and forearms on the BOSU.

2. Lift entire body off the ground until it forms a straight line from head to toe, resting on forearms and toes.

3. Hold for desired length of time keeping chin tucked and back flat.

Planking on BOSU single leg

1. Lie prone on the floor with feet together and hands on the BOSU.
2. Lift entire body off the ground until it forms a straight line from head to toe, resting on hands and toes.
3. Lift one leg.
4. Hold for desired length of time, keeping chin tucked and back flat.

Adaptation: single leg plank can be performed on exercise mat or on floor.

Stability ball plank

1. Get into plank position by supporting your body weight with your chest and forearms on the ball and your toes on the floor.
2. Lift your chest off the ball so your upper body weight is supported by your forearms.
3. Keep your abdominals contracted and your back straight while keeping your back flat.
4. Hold for desired length on time while maintaining balance.

Other balancing ideas:

- **Bubbles.** Also recommended by our occupational therapist, this activity involves blowing bubbles and asking children to stand still and pop the bubbles with the pointer finger of their dominant hand (the one they use for writing). This means they will have to reach across the midline to pop bubbles, which is the "point"!

- **Pick-up-sticks.** A traditional game my children love to play, recommended by our occupational therapist as good for treating cross-dominance.

- **Jacks.** Another traditional game good for crossing the midline.

- **Clapping games.** These are similar to "Patty Cake" and with younger children, I just make them up to fit the rhythm of a fun song. When done with a partner, the pattern should be something like "Down, clap, cross (clap hands with partner), clap, down" etc. Older students have a lot of fun making up their own and teaching their "moves" to the rest of us! More of these ideas can be found at http://www.teacher-support-force. com/brainexercises.html

Key Points to Remember

- Improving balance and coordination have shown to improve academics.

- Reading problems can be a physical issue related to coordination across the midline of the body.

- Physically active children often lack coordination and balance.

- Improved balance and coordination prevent injuries.

- Basic skills like cutting with scissors or writing can be improved with balance and coordination activities.

Activities for Fun and Play

"Everything children need to learn they can – and should – learn through play. Indeed, play is the vehicle through which children acquire information about themselves and the world around them. One of the most misguided notions regarding early childhood education right now is that play is 'frivolous' and that 'real' learning involves sitting. It's nonsense."

Rae Pica

As I mentioned in Chapter 1, recess was one of my fondest memories of school. But it was about more than just burning off excess energy. Recess was where I learned to socialize with other students, including girls. I also learned about important traits like cooperation, to take turns, friendship, trust, and many other skills that can't easily be measured on a standardized test, but are invaluable for surviving in the real world.

Unfortunately, with such a focus on standardized testing, recess and playtime are slowly, quickly in some cases, a thing of the past. Keeping students in from recess is even used as a punishment for an overactive child in class. Here, again, if a child is "fidgeting" in class, does anyone really think it's a good idea to take away the time where he can actually run around and burn up some of that energy? Students need "brain breaks," where we give the gray matter time to process information learned while allowing the body to move and burn off energy.

How many times have you seen the USA compared to Finland or another country in relation to test scores? But did you know that countries like Finland and France focus a lot of valuable school time on recess and play? That's right: students in these countries spend over an hour each day in recess and play. In fact, in Finland, students are given a 15-minute recess break every hour. That is a far cry from the time spent here in the US, where many districts have cut out recess entirely to make more time for learning. I hate to break the news to these educators who should know better, but *play is learning*! So, while your school may not allow formal recess, you can incorporate short breaks throughout the day for your students. Most schools with recess usually allow only one per day, which is not enough to really benefit students.

Tim Walker was an American teacher who traveled to Finland to teach 5th grade. He has recounted several times how he tried to extend the learning time in his classes to cover more content, rather than taking a 15-minute break every hour. He said his students would quickly become disengaged and almost zombielike after 90-minute sessions. So, he decided to embrace the 15-minute recess every hour, and after 45 minutes of teaching, his students would get 15 minutes of recess like all the other students. He said the transformation was immediate. After the 15-minute breaks, the students would come into the classroom with a bounce in their step and would be ready to focus on work! And remember that Finnish students consistently score higher than the USA on PISA tests. Could this nugget of information be one of the diamonds in the rough that could change how educating children moves forward?

Unfortunately, in the USA, the trend is to do away with recess because it is seen as a waste of time. Besides taking recess away from students who misbehave, there is also a trend to send students for extra help in academic areas during recess if they are behind. This only makes the student hate school worse, because there is no joy or fun to learning. You may be wondering, how is removing recess working out here in the USA? Well, the first eye-opener came with the National Center for Research study, that showed obesity among children has tripled since the 1980s, which is the same time that public education began to cut recess from our schools. Just a coincidence? Hardly! Their study concluded that children who are more active in school tend to do more physical activities after school, such as county and recreational sports leagues. The elimination of recess is also affecting students' performances. While the No Child Left Behind Act was created to boost test efficiency scores, students' grades are going in the opposite direction. The grade deficiencies can easily be related to the cutting back of physical activity time during school hours. Spending all hours of the day sitting in a classroom is not ideal, or even natural, for a young student.

Since academics are the driving force behind many schools' decisions, guess what the research shows when it comes to recess and playtime for children? You guessed it! Recess and playtime actually improve achievement levels for students rather than lower them. Researchers in the Netherlands report that children who are more active, whether at school or on their own, tend to have higher GPAs and better scores on standardized tests. In a review of 14 studies that looked at physical activity and academic performance, investigators found that the more children moved, the better their grades were in school, particularly in the basic subjects of math, English and reading. The bottom line is that there is a brain-body connection that benefits active students academically.

Other recent studies have shown that to have a break, or breaks, for physical activity during the school day is more beneficial to test scores than the normal sedentary learning that occurs. The physical activity breaks, recess, and even playtime also strengthen memory skills and vocabulary skills for younger children. The break from the classroom has been shown to be extremely beneficial for children with special needs and diagnosed attention deficit disorders. It allows them to let free their physical tensions and clear their mind. And children need time to free their minds. After recess, these children have proven to be less restless and more focused on the task at hand, just as the teacher in Finland affirmed. Imagine if you were training an athlete, would you have her run sprints all day long, or have her run sprints and then take breaks to recover? Obviously you would take breaks to let the muscles recover, right? Well, guess what? The brain is a muscle and it needs time to recover and refocus as well. The brain actually needs down time to process and store information more effectively. So make sure to take *brain breaks* during the day for students to have fun, get moving, and learn more!

With the focus on high-stakes testing, we forget learning can and should be active and even fun. Learning can be enjoyable and satisfying even when it requires work. Much like your job, learning is hard work, but at the end of the day the work produces a sense of satisfaction. Remember: as adults we try new activities that we find fun, engaging, or of value to us. We don't typically participate in activities that we don't like or find useful to our lives. Why do we expect children to be any different?

Children are also very social beings that need to develop their interpersonal skills. They naturally do this through play. These skills are all but ignored in education today, and yet we continue to wonder why students are disrespectful, act like bullies, and can have a hard time developing healthy relationships with teachers and peers. Ultimately the skills that are required for today's culture include respect, responsibility, and the building of intentional relationships. Part of the challenge of instilling these skills in today's classroom is that we want the "quick fix," and there is no "quick remedy" for some concerns. The students have to be given time to work within groups or teams and to interact with peers. This type of work will model play and allow them the chance to build these interpersonal skills.

Another aspect of developing interpersonal skills requires the students have time to actually interact socially. Unfortunately, opportunities such as recess are distant memories in many school systems. Why? So we can make more time for testing or more lessons on how to read? Some schools take recess time away for bad behavior. We will reiterate this throughout the book: NEVER punish students by taking away recess or social time at lunch! In fact, while many teachers think this is an acceptable form of punishment, I see it more like cruel and unusual punishment. In fact, remember when I got the spanking for skipping down the hall? Well, I would have rather gotten the spanking than to have had recess taken away or to have had silent lunch! And, ironically, if it weren't for recess, I would have probably gotten spankings every week or possibly been diagnosed with ADHD myself. Yes it may be a little easier and quieter to make children sit in desk or silently at lunch, but what is in the best interest of the students? When is the last time we really sought to understand what is best for the growth and development of children?

A major longitudinal study published in *Pediatrics*, conducted by researchers at the Albert Einstein College of Medicine, focused on the recess or playtime allowed for 11,000 students. The results showed that children with more than 15 minutes of recess a day showed better behavior in class than those who had little or none. "We need to understand that kids need a break," Dr. Romina Barros, who conducted the study (Barros, Silver, & Stein, 2009), said. "Our brains can concentrate and pay attention for 45 to 60 minutes, and in kids it's even less. For them to be able to acquire all the academic skills we want them to learn, they need a break to go out and release the energy and play and be social." This research alone shows that kids need a break not only to move and burn off energy, but it is necessary for them to process information as well.

Regrettably, this study also revealed that children exposed to none or minimal recess were much more likely to be from families with lower incomes and lower levels of education, to live in large cities, and to be from the Northeast or South. Now, imagine if these students had 15 minutes per hour rather than per day. There would more than likely be an even greater drop in misbehavior. What teacher doesn't want improved behavior in the classroom? You would accomplish much more academically in less time with adequate recess!

Remember: students instinctively want to discover and learn, so let's provide them the opportunity to succeed, not simply on a test, but in life. Remember the old adage of "Work hard, play hard." Let's do both in the classroom. Here are some examples:

- Exercise play (aerobics, running, chasing, dance routines).
- Rough-and-tumble play (soccer, football, wrestling).
- Solitary play (doing puzzles, object manipulation).
- Outdoor learning activities (digging, observing insects).
- Stand and stretch activities (tai chi, "Simon Says").
- Constructive play (building with blocks, model-building).
- Functional play (purposeful play, core, balance training).
- Group noncompetitive games (examples in the Ideas to Try section).
- Individual competitive games (marbles, track and field, hopscotch).
- Adventure or confidence play (ropes courses, trust walks).
- Group noncompetitive activities (dance, drama).
- Walking excursions (outdoors, indoors).

Play is another aspect of education and recess that has but been abandoned in pursuit of test preparation. However, like recess, play has been scientifically proved to be good for the brain. All animals play, even though playing is not immediately productive and is sometimes dangerous. Yet grizzly bears that play the most survive longest. Rats that socialize more with other rats develop bigger, more complex brains. And play stimulates nerve growth in the portions of the brain that process emotions and executive function.

The social aspects of play can't be overlooked, either. Rough-and-tumble play teaches us how to cooperate and play fair. Research in humans and animals has shown that roughhousing is necessary for the development of social awareness, cooperation, fairness, and altruism. This is particularly true for preschoolers: what looks like anarchy on the playground is an experiment in the give-and-take necessary for the mastery of social skills. One researcher found that early forms of play, such as chasing, relate to social problem-solving skills that children develop later on. And, if young rats are denied rough-and-tumble play, they develop serious social problems in adulthood and aren't able to mate. When we deny, especially boys, the ability to develop these skills, then we can understand why they disrupt in class, misbehave, and other issues. It's because we aren't letting them be children.

We simply cannot let recess and play be taken out of schools. As **Rae Pica** explained, "First, parents and teachers have to advocate—and advocate fiercely—to keep physical education and recess in the schools! They can arm themselves with information from organizations like the American Association for the Child's Right to Play [www.ipausa.com]."

Ideas to Try

- **Name Five.** The ability to have students sit or stand in a circle is needed for Name Five and one prop … anything can be used for this prop, as long as it doesn't matter if it gets broken and as long as it is easily passed from one person to another. I like using one of those cheap trick or treat pumpkins because its lightweight, fees like a ball, and makes a loud noise when you pop it with your hand. The objective is not to be the one stuck in the middle (literally: one person has to begin the game—ideally the teacher—standing in the middle of the circle). In order to get out of the middle, that person, holding the object (pumpkin), approaches anyone in the circle and tells them to (let's say it is a history class) "Name five dead presidents"—and then hands the pumpkin to the person they just gave the directive to. That person must immediately say either "Accept" or "Reject" and then immediately pass the pumpkin to the person to their left. If he said "Accept," he must then name five dead presidents while the rest of the class are passing the pumpkin around the circle as fast as they possibly can without skipping anyone. If the pumpkin makes it back to the person before he can name the five dead presidents, he must take his turn in the middle, and the person in the middle gets to take his seat. If he says "Reject," then the person in the middle who told him to name the five dead presidents will have to do it themselves before the pumpkin makes it back to the original person he handed it to. The more people in the circle, the more challenging the number would need to be. It makes for a good review time of any subject matter, twisted with a bit of fun as well. Inevitable movement comes into play with the excitement of whether or not the person is going to be able to do it.

- **Plates.** Have kids all put a paper plate on their head. Have them move about the room. If their plate falls, they are frozen and someone else has to bend down without having their plate fall off their head and put it on a classmate's head. The object is to keep everyone in the game.

- **Heads up, seven up.** Seven kids are up in front of the classroom and all others have their heads on their desks with their thumbs up. Each of the seven taps one person and they put their thumb down. Once all students choose one person, you say, "Heads up, seven up." Those seven stand and try to figure out who picked them.

- **Cross-lateral moves.** Have the kids move by doing cross-lateral things such as touching the left shoulder or knee with the right hand, etc.

- **Imaginary energy ball.** Besides physical activity, we also limit students' opportunities to be creative. This game allows students and teacher to use their imaginations and get active at the same time. I like throwing an imaginary energy ball around for brain breaks—the kind of invisible ball that you have to really cup with both your hands, or else it will escape and go crazy and destroy everything in its path (demonstrating, with a student you know will play along with you really well, appropriate tossing and catching techniques, e.g., shaking cupped hands, then tossing like a basketball, football, frisbee, whatever, and catching in any creative way you like, e.g., in a shirt pocket, behind the back, in an ear) ... and then just pass it around the room until everyone has had a turn or two, and when someone finally passes it back to me and I see the need to end the game.

- **Physical challenges.** Challenge students to do something physically difficult, such as standing on one foot with arms extended or this one: grab your nose with left hand and grab your left earlobe with your right hand, then quickly switch so that your right hand is on your nose and your left hand is grabbing your right earlobe. Yoga poses could also be a good variation.

- **Scavenger hunts.** Scavenger hunts are a lot of fun, but they definitely take some planning to get set up. The great thing is, they can be used for nearly every subject. I like to set up a scavenger hunt for when starting new social studies, science, or reading units. I go through the material beforehand and I create questions, fill-in-the-blank, pictures, dates, people—anything that I want my students to really know before we get into the unit. And then I put them into small groups and they have to search the textbooks, encyclopedias, online, and around the classroom for the clues.

- **Wave Stretch.** Teacher script: "I can tell you guys need a little break, so I'm going to give you a chance to get up and stretch. We're going to do an activity called 'Wave Stretch.' Let's stand in a circle. We're going to start with me—when I do my stretch, just like at a Braves game when the fans do the wave, the person beside me will then, too, do my stretch and we will all hold that stretch until it has moved all the way around the circle and back to me. When it reaches me, Billy here, standing to my left, will change the stretch to any other stretch he chooses (as long as it is something possible for everyone to do)—at which time we will do the wave again, changing my stretch to his. We will do this until everyone has had a chance to change the stretch."

  A drama teacher, literature teacher—or any natural storyteller might want to do what I call "Story Stretch." Everybody in a circle. First person (25 words or less) begins the story with "Once upon a time ..." and as he is telling the story he is putting movement into it with his body that everyone else has to copy for example, "Once upon a time there were 10 teenagers who went hiking through the woods, and they saw a bear ..." (motions for hiking and reactions to seeing bear). Then the next person adds on to the story, and so on until the last person, who ends it with a big "The End" ...

- **Dog shake.** "OK, we're all going to walk in an orderly fashion as though we are the most serious people in the world, to the exit door of the building. When we all get outside, let's say about 20 feet away from the possibility of any other foot traffic, we are all going to simultaneously shake like a dog who has just gotten out of the water for a minimum of 30 seconds—or you can say a minute, which do you want: 30 seconds or a minute? OK. And then, as though nothing unusual has happened, we are going to form a nice rigid, self-controlled line and walk back to the room. If you all can make it back to the room with serious faces—no smiles; we're here to learn something—I'll make sure to find time to do more out-of-the-box activities with you. Are you up for this? OK—get your game face on, and let's make a line...."

- **Educational bingo.** There are literally countless ways to use bingo. I created an award-winning bingo game based upon the people of American history. The boards have people's faces on them and the clues are all standards-based facts. What about math bingo in which the boards have numbers and the clues are problems that the students have to do mentally (or with scratch paper). Bingo can be used for phonics, vocabulary, spelling, letter sounds ...

- **Around the World.** This might be my favorite time-filler, and a quick game. Around the World works best with a set of flashcards—can be math, vocab, sight words, or spelling. You have all your students stand up, the first student stands next to the student behind them. You show a flashcard, and whoever is the fastest to say the correct answer moves on. The idea is to be the best in the whole class. For a bonus, if a student makes it all the way around the room, then they get to go against you. They *love* this. "Since you're the teacher, give them three tries to beat me. If they beat you, then the next time you play around the world they get to be the 'teacher'."

- **Spelling baseball.**

  1. Split the class into two teams.

  2. Designate where the "bases" are in your classroom.

  3. Students take turns spelling words; if they are correct, they advance a base.

  4. If they misspell the word, they go to the back of the line.

  5. See how many home runs can be scored in two minutes, then switch teams.

- **Animal roundup.** Get group members silently to think of their favorite animal. Then tell group members that, without talking, they need to arrange themselves from largest to smallest animals. Group members can only make gestures and the noise of their animal. After they have finished, have group members go around and say the animal they were supposed to be to see if it was accurate.

- **Brain break (pen flip).**

  1. Stand up.

  2. Take a pen and flip it *one revolution*. (Imagine a piece of tape on one end of the pen, then throw the pen from the tape side. Have the pen go one full turn around to get to the tape side again.)

  3. Do the same thing with your other hand.

  4. Get a pen for both hands and try to do both pens at the same time.

5. If you really are good at that, now try to throw the pens up into the air and catch them in opposite hands. This is tough.

- **Be sure to have logical consequences** if someone does not follow a rule. (If a student does not follow lab rules, then they only observe and do not actively participate in the lab. They don't lose recess time. The consequence must match the behavior.)

- **Drop everything and play.** Remember the drop-everything-and-read initiative? Well, I always incorporated a drop everything and play. Remember the motto, "Work hard and play hard"? Well, I made sure my students understood this as more than just a quote. I got the idea from coaching youth football many years ago. The head coach would call off practice every few weeks and would make the practice time a study hall, where we actually worked with the students on schoolwork, or occasionally he would make it a play day. We would bring water balloons, shaving cream, bring food, and have a party instead of practice. The athletes loved it and it proved to be a great break to reinvigorate them. So, once every few weeks I would take my class and either play a game or simply make it a study hall where they could work in groups on classwork or another subject in which they needed help. The students loved this "break" from the rigor of academics and it really did seem to reinvigorate them!

Key Points to Remember

- Playing *is* learning.
- Recess has a positive impact on academic achievement.
- Students listen better after recess and are more focused in class.
- Recess has a beneficial effect on children's social development.
- Brain breaks help the brain process information, while allowing the body to burn up excess energy.
- Recess improves children's well-being overall.
- Recess and playtime increase caloric expenditure, which can help deter sedentary obesity.
- High-achieving countries like Finland allow 15 minutes of recess every hour!

Activities for Real-World STEM Instruction

12

"STEM offers jobs that are active, so STEM courses should be taught in a similar manner. Not just note taking and tests. Do students really hate math or simply hate how it's taught?"

Aleta Margolis (founder of Inspired Teaching)

STEM classes have become a big focus in education in recent years. Although trying to get students interested in science and math are not new to education, they have been a focus since the Race to Space of the 1960s.

Now, the President's Council of Advisors on Science and Technology has called for an increase in funding for STEM (science, technology, engineering, and math) to provide 100,000 new jobs in these fields over the next 10 years, as well as to get more girls to pursue degrees in these fields.

The shortage of employees in STEM fields may have little to do with the fields themselves, but may have more to do with how the subjects have been taught. A recent study suggests that active learning leads to increases in examination performance that would raise average grades by a half a letter, and that failure rates under traditional lecturing increase by 55 percent over the rates observed under active learning. The analysis supports theory claiming that calls to increase the number of students receiving STEM degrees could be answered, at least in part, by abandoning traditional lecturing in favor of active learning.

This research suggests that active learning is critical for success in STEM classes. Active learning was defined in the research as engaging students in the process of learning through activities and/or discussion in class, as opposed to passively listening to an expert. It emphasizes higher-order thinking and often involves group work. But, what if physical activity and actual team building were also integrated into the equation? Would there be even more retention of information and increase in test scores? Think of how children may view math, science, or even engineering, if learning were more active?

Imagine if a sport like basketball, or even music, were only taught by lecture and note taking? There would be much less interest in them. If music appreciation involved only note taking and tests, I doubt if very many students would actually appreciate music. But actively participating and learning the subjects is what makes them more appealing. Maybe it's time to rethink how we teach the STEM courses such as math so that students find them more interactive, engaging, and applicable to the real world.

It would only make sense that STEM classes should include actual hands-on activities related to their field. I remember taking a woodshop class when I was in school. While the first few projects were rudimentary, by the end of the year we were making projects like birdhouses and breadboxes that we were actually proud of constructing. We could actually see the progress we had made over the course of the year, rather than just assume we had learned something. So, if we are talking about engineering, for example, shouldn't students actually be engaged in active learning rather than just taking notes and being tested over information? Actually jobs in the STEM fields are jobs of action and innovation, not theory, so how we teach them should reflect the real world. Engaging in projects, team building, and active learning will allow students to find relevance in subjects that they typically see as abstract or irrelevant.

Aleta Margolis, the founder of Inspired Teaching, made the point during an interview with us that physical activity would benefit STEM classes. He said:

> We include teaching pedagogy in physical education classes, so why shouldn't we include physical activity in the academic classroom? For example, people in the STEM fields are not sitting at desks all day, they are out actually being active. Such as a scientist wading in a pond because they are an environmental scientist. These are the types of active learning that we need to include in our academic classes so students can make the connection to the real world and they may find out they like these content areas better when the learning is real.

And what would be wrong with creating a more active learning environment for a class like math? Aleta further explained:

Have you ever wondered why so many children hate math or at least claim to hate math? Memorizing functions, formulas, and theories to simply figure out equations is not exactly exciting! But, what if there were more application of the subject in the classroom. Instead of simply memorizing the Pythagorean to answer a worksheet question, what if the students had to use formula to figure out the hypotenuse using two walls in the classroom or hallway? Or, for fractions, a great opportunity is when students are getting ready for lunch. Let half-class line up, while half of class gets jackets, and then have half of them clean off tables. Or do a circle with like 24 students. Ask one third to step inside of circle, which will be eight. Then ask half of them to sit down. This will be four people. This shows how simple fractions actually work. There are so many ways to include real-world examples naturally that help students understand the relevance of the topic.

Dr. Spyridoula Vazou, Assistant Professor of Exercise Psychology and Pedagogy in the Department of Kinesiology at Iowa State University, shared in our interview that

Children may develop a negative attitude towards STEM not only because of the difficulty of the material and their low perceived competence for these academic subjects, but also due to their lack of motivation during instruction (as a result of sitting for prolonged periods of time without being engaged during instruction). In my studies, we have found that integrating physical activity with academics increased students' perceived competence and enjoyment of math, both acutely (compared to traditional lessons) and after an eight-week intervention. Importantly, both enjoyment and perceived competence were significant predictors of math performance after the intervention, even after controlling for baseline math performance. These findings show that, by integrating physical activity with academics, students are more engaged and interested in math and their performance improves, likely as a result of both the physiological effects of exercise and the increased motivation for learning.

In one research study, students in 3rd through 6th grades had access to exercise equipment with TV monitors. For instance, a treadmill had a monitor that played geography lessons as the student ran through the scene, and a rock-climbing wall was outfitted with numbers that changed as they climbed to help students work on math skills. Researchers compared state standardized reading test scores for the year before and the year after initiation of the program. Each student took standardized tests in the fall and spring. In the fall, the results included an individualized goal for each student to reach on the spring test. Researchers measured the number of students who met or exceeded their goal score in the spring. Results showed that the time spent out of a traditional classroom in order to increase physical education did not hurt students' academic achievement but that the student test scores actually improved. Specifically, the percentage of students reaching their goal on the state tests increased from 55 percent before the program was started to 68.5 percent after the program was initiated. If any other program offered such gains, schools would be scrambling to incorporate it.

Educational expert **Rae Pica** believes that STEM classes need to be more active and connected to the real world for students to truly appreciate them. As she stated,

> I'm in favor of active learning regardless of the content area being explored. Young children, especially, need to physically experience concepts in order to understand them. They have to get into high and low positions to really comprehend the quantitative concepts of high and low. They have stand next to, far from, over, in front of, and behind objects to grasp these early geometry concepts. They need to experiment at water tables with objects of varying weights and densities to discover information about flotation. They have to build with Legos to explore engineering concepts. All of these concepts are better experienced through physical experiences—through active learning—than through books and worksheets!

Rebeca Plantier (Founder of Fit to Inspire and Huffington Post blogger) shared in our interview how math is often taught in France to incorporate activity. She explains:

> In France, more recently, there has been a shift in teaching mathematics from traditional notetaking on theory, and applied exercises followed by class-wide correction to a "complex task" model in which students are rendered active in group or pair work and sometimes individually as graded homework. The students are given short missions in which mental gymnastics between geometry, arithmetic, and algebra are required in order to solve problems they could potentially encounter in the real

world. They could, for example, be asked to compare the prices of different packets of notebooks in various supermarkets. The skills required to accomplish these missions are as much mathematical as humanistic, since partnership, compromise, and deduction are necessary. Although many teachers still use conventional methods, this shift has sparked a realization that a hands-on approach is more effective in engaging students in making them the center of learning, instead of recipients meant to be filled with knowledge.

One way to make STEM classes more realistic is to incorporate project-based learning (PBL), which is a teaching method where students gain knowledge and skills by working for an extended period of time to investigate and respond to an engaging and complex question, problem, or challenge. This type of learning often creates a finished project that can be seen, heard, or experienced. This type of learning reflects real world application.

Much like team building, which we discuss in Chapter 7, PBL breaks students out of the mold of sitting in a desk and learning material in isolation. When we think about working in the real world, most corporations are looking for people who can work on teams, and more often than not it is to complete projects. Too often, work done in schools is filed in the garbage as soon as it has been graded. If our work as adults was immediately filed in the trash, we may not be as engaging, either. But most of our work deals with completing projects, whether it is constructing a building, creating a new product, or even an advertisement campaign for a company.

The projects we assign in school don't have to be that complex; they can be simpler projects that young students can handle. When I taught middle grades, I would always incorporate simple PBL in my science classes. I actually had students work on projects in groups and then teach the class. For example, if we were learning about microscopic animals, I would have the students design a microscope and create an advertisement for it. They would have to create a budget, target audience, and how they would market it all within a certain time in history. This meant they also had to research costs, methods of advertising and other aspects which would include math, history, and even technology. The students would then create and brand the new product and share their ad campaign.

Another topic that I did for older students was to create a service project where they would raise money and food for a local food bank. I allowed them to research the needs of the food bank, design a campaign, and then allowed them to deliver the food and work at the food bank for a day. I was beyond proud when the campaign raised over 4,000 lb of food for the food bank. Several of the students continued to volunteer at the food bank on weekends or evenings because it made such an impact on them.

Some projects are actually real-world problems, such as a teacher was in a fender bender in the parking lot. She had her class come up with designs to make the parking lot safer and traffic flow better. Another project that I have used was to have students design lunch menus for the school. They would have to use a budget, make sure the food was healthy, tasty, and met the recommended daily allowance of nutrients. This is one that could be very relevant for students and the school if some menus were chosen to be implemented. At the very least you could have students bring in the winning foods and have your own healthy but tasty lunch during the class period.

Finally, STEM classes don't have to be boring and they don't have to be taught in isolation. Most careers in the STEM fields are jobs of action, and when students can experience the real-world application of these fields, then they not only see the relevance but may find that they actually do love science, and even math!

Ideas to Try

- **Math Olympics.** As part of a measurement unit, hold a Math Olympics in your classroom. You begin with an opening ceremony that includes a parade of athletes and the running of the torch. Then you can set up stations that students rotate through. These stations include a javelin throw (straw), discus throw (paper plate), shot put (cotton ball), high jump, and long jump. Students work in pairs to help each other with the measuring. This can take place in one day or over the course of a week. At the end of the day or week, conclude with an award ceremony. You can even play the National Anthem and give students their medals.

- **Save the pond/park/stream campaign.** Take students to a stream or a pond in the woods and examine the ecosystem around it. Then have the students divide up into groups and get them to design a "Save the pond" campaign. Focus could be on animals that survive because of the pond, pollution of the pond, and even recreation for public that could be created around the pond. I have had classes in the past actually clean up around streams and ponds themselves during class, and even after school as part of volunteer efforts.

- **Math & Movement**™**.** This is a kinesthetic, multisensory approach to teaching math that incorporates physical exercise, stretching, cross-body movements, yoga, and visually pleasing floor mats designed to encourage students to practice math concepts. The Math & Movement™ program allows students to physically hop, walk, crawl, dance, or touch the mats and banners as they learn, thus using more learning modalities (visual, auditory, motor, and kinesthetic) when practicing. For more information, see www.mathandmovement.com/

- **Orienteering Scavenger Hunt.** *Purpose*: The students will take a reading with a compass and use the compass to reach multiple checkpoints.

  Prerequisites: Traveling, directions such as north, south, east, and west.

  Materials needed: Compasses (one for every student), one demonstration compass (either large one or overhead), balloons, poly spots, and direction cards. Detailed instructions on the activity can be found at www.pecentral.org/lessonideas/ViewLesson.asp?ID=2983

- **Nature walks.** One of the best activities to be physically active and learn is to take nature walks. When I taught middle grades, I would take my class outside at least once a week. Whether we were learning about plants, trees, animals, insects, or even fungi, we would take a nature walk and experience everything firsthand. This is also a great time to get water samples, leaves, etc. to examine in the classroom. Many schools are connected to parks, ball fields, or wooded areas where most of the items can be found. Even a nearby walking path is a great way to experience the woods while keeping the students from getting dirty or muddy.

- **Vocabulary relay.** During this activity the class is divided into teams. This can work with as many teams as the teacher can create. The ideal number of students per team is four. Each team will also need a place to write on the board. In my class I usually have four teams of four students, with the front whiteboard sectioned off into four parts, one for each team. Each team is given a stack of vocabulary cards with only the definitions on them. Focus on vocabulary a specific STEM class, or use vocabulary associated with the STEM field. A key aspect to this is to number each card. I usually use different-colored cards for each team and write the number on one side with the definition on the other. This keeps the sets separate and allows for the terms to be randomly written and ensures one team cannot look to another for the answer. I also have an answer key already generated for each team set of cards. To play the game, the first person reads the definition and then runs to the board to write the term. The student runs back and passes on the deck. The next person reads the next definition and runs to the board to write the answer. This continues until all of the terms have been written. The team to finish first gets four bonus points; the second, three; third, two; and last, one bonus point. Then we all sit down and go over the answers. Two points are given for every correct answer and one point is deducted for an incorrect answer. Then the bonus points are added in. The students hang on every answer to learn the points total. This really helps reviewing, because the students are really paying attention!

- **Create learning stations.** In science class we have station labs where students move around and participate in different activities at each lab table. In writers' workshop, students have various stations, such as a publishing station, an editing station, and a private workstation.

- **52 card pickup.** *Target*: This warm-up activity gets students moving while helping them to practice their mathematical skills.

   Materials: A deck of playing cards.

   To begin this activity, have students form pairs and each person picks up a playing card found in the middle of the room. Once the students have a playing card, together with their partner they will decide what station to go to based on the suits of their playing cards. For example, if one person has hearts as their suit and their partner has diamonds, the two of them have to decide as a team to go to either the hearts station or the diamonds station. If both people in a group have clubs, they can only go to the clubs station.

   At each station, students are required to do the activity that is listed. For example, at the hearts station students would be required to do 10 jumping jacks. After each pair decides which station they are going to, the teacher will call out either to add, subtract, or multiply the pair's cards together. Once the pair has come up with their number, they will see if that is the highest number amongst the other pairs at their station. If it is the highest number, then that pair only has to do half the amount of work that is required. For example, instead of doing 10 jumping jacks, the pair would only have to do five. Everyone else would have to do 10 jumping jacks at the station. After a pair finishes at a station, they will return their playing cards to the center of the room and each person selects another card. This activity is then repeated.

Adaptations: Allow each station to be adapted to the needs of special children. For instance, one station could be where students practice shooting hoops. This would allow students using wheelchairs to participate.

Key Points to Remember

- STEM jobs are active, so classes should include active learning.

- Students perform better in STEM courses with hands-on activities rather than lectures.

- Students may not actually hate the subject; they just dislike how it's taught.

- Allow students to create projects that can be seen, heard, and shared.

- Use real-world problems for math or science.

- Incorporate physical fitness into the class when possible.

Afterword

"Nothing happens until something moves."

Albert Einstein

As the research in the book suggests, education has done a great disservice to children over the past generation. We have spent billions of dollars and initiated thousands of programs, and the only increases we have seen are increased behavior issues, increased students on medications, and increased health issues such as obesity. Sadly, the one area where increase is desirable, achievement, has steadily declined. We have simply missed the mark when it comes to teaching children in the manner in which they learn. One look at school life in Finland or other countries and we see stark contrast in recess, physical activity, and other factors that affect student achievement.

One reason this must be addressed by our educational system is that students spend more waking hours at school than they do at home. Students do better when they participate in physical activities outside of school, but imagine the improvement they could experience if it were ingrained into the school day as well. Our bodies were designed to move, explore, and be active. Sitting for long periods of time is not natural to children, and it negatively affects our bodies to be still for long periods of time. Unfortunately, as we shared in the beginning of the book, many expert educators see recess, physical activity, and play as a waste of valuable learning time. But, as the evidence overwhelmingly supports, it is through play, physical activity, and movement that children actually learn best.

Even though schools may have cut back on recess, playtime, and physical activity in schools, all hope is not lost. The good news is that you can incorporate physical activity and play into your own classroom. With all the activities shared throughout the book, you can implement as many as you feel comfortable. The key to remember is that physical activity and play can indeed be incorporated throughout the class to reduce stress, increase focus and strength, improve teamwork, and ultimately improve student achievement.

For our final thought, I (Melody) would like to share one success story that you as teachers can relate to as adults and as educators. A few years ago, I challenged my coauthor Brad to train with me. We had been friends for a few years and while he was a former athlete and still trained. However, with his busy schedule of teaching, speaking, and writing, I knew he didn't focus on training like he should. I also knew that he neglected working his core strength and balance when he did train.

I developed a program that focused on many of the core and balance exercises that we have shared in this book. In less than five months of focusing on developing his core strength and balance, he lost nearly 50 pounds of weight. He shared that he felt so much better, felt more focused, and had more energy than he had in years.

Over the course of the next year, then, we began to collaborate on workshops with schools and with young athletes. These exercises aren't just sound in theory, but they have been successful with adults as well as children. The exercises we have prescribed require the mind and body to work in unison for maximum benefits. And, in the case of students, the benefits include improved focus and achievement as well.

Our ideas eventually became the foundation for this book, which can help transform education, because we know our children are worth it. Every child deserves the opportunity to develop physically and mentally to maximize their potential in school and life. Let's provide the next generation of learners the greatest service we can provide by letting them learn not on their seats, but on their feet!

Sources

Alber, R. (2015). Back to School: Rules and Routines in the Classroom. *Edutopia* September 3. Retrieved from http://www.edutopia.org/blog/rules-routines-school-year-start-classroom-management

Armstrong, T. (1999). *ADD/ADHD Alternatives in the Classroom*. Alexandria, VA: ASCD.

Barros, R., Silver, E., & Stein, R. (2009). School Recess and Group Classroom Behavior. *Pediatrics*, 123(2), pp. 431–436. doi: 10.1542/peds.2007-2825

Benden, M., Blake, J. J., Wendel, M. L. & Huber, J. C. (2011). The Impact of Stand-Biased Desks in Classrooms on Calorie Expenditure in Children. *American Journal of Public Health* 101(8) (August), pp. 1433–1436. doi: 10.2105/AJPH.2010.30007

Brewer, C. (1995). *Music and Learning: Seven ways to use music in the classroom*. Tucson, AZ: Zephyr Press.

Bright, R. (n.d.). Kids Who Can't Sit Still: Letting them fidget may keep students focused on learning. *NEA*. Retrieved from http://www.nea.org/tools/47003.htm

Chaddick, L., & Erickson, K. L. (2010). Basal Ganglia Volume is Associated with Aerobic Fitness in Preadolescent Children. *Developmental Neuroscience*, 32(3) (August), pp. 249–256. doi: 10.1159/000316648

Deardorff, J. (2015). The Best Brain Exercise May Be Physical. *Chicago Tribune*. Retrieved from http://www.chicagotribune.com/lifestyles/health/sc-hlth-0506-exercise-for-the-brain-20150430-story.html

Eckerd, M., & Rudin, S. (n.d.). Improving Executive-Function Skills Can Help Your ADHD Child Overcome Frustrating Academic Obstacles and Succeed in School. *Attitude Magazine.* Retrieved from http://www. additudemag.com/adhd/article/8392.html

Evans, J. K. (n.d.) How Does Integrating Music and Movement in a Kindergarten Classroom Affect Student Achievement in Math? Unpublished paper, Wayne State College, Wayne, NE.

Fedewa, A. L., & Erwin, H. E. (2011). Stability Balls and Students with Attention and Hyperactivity Concerns: Implications for on-task and in-seat behavior. *American Journal of Occupational Therapy,* 65 (July/August), pp. 393–399. doi: 10.5014/ajot.2011.000554

Freeman, E., Eddy, S., McDonough, M., Smith, M. K., Okroafor, N., Jordt, H., et al. (2013). Active Learning Increases Student Performance in Science, Engineering, and Mathematics. *Proceedings of the National Academy of Sciences,* 111(23), pp. 8410–8415. doi: 10.1073/pnas.1319030111

Gunter, E. (1993). *Superlearning 2000: The new technologies of self-empowerment.* New York, NY: Milligan Books.

Hannaford, C. (2008). *Smart Moves: Why Learning is Not All in Your Head.* Salt Lake City, UT: Great River Books.

Henley, J., & McBride, J. (2007). Robbing Elementary Students of Their Childhood: The Perils of No Child Left Behind. *Education,* 128(1), pp. 56–63.

Hillman, C. H., Erickson K. I., & Kramer, A. F. (2008). Be Smart, Exercise Your Heart: Exercise effects on brain and cognition. *National Review of Neuroscience,* 9, pp. 58–65. doi: 10.1038/nrn2298

Jensen, E., (2005). *Teaching with the Brain in Mind.* Alexandria, VA: ASCD.

Jolly, A. (2014). Six Characteristics of a Great STEM Lesson. *Education Week.* Retrieved from http://www.edweek.org/tm/articles/2014/06/17/ctq_jolly_stem.html

King, K., & Scahill, C. (2011). Combining Physical Activity with Classroom Lessons Results in Improved Test Scores. *American Academy of Pediatrics,* news release.

Lang, H. C., & Scheffler, R. M. (2010). The Discrepancy in Attention Deficit Hyperactivity Disorder (ADHD) Medications Diffusion: 1994–2003—a global pharmaceutical data analysis. *Health Policy,* 97(1) (September), pp. 71–78. doi: 10.1016/j.healthpol.2010.03.005

Lin, F., & Zhou, Y. (2012). Abnormal White Matter Integrity in Adolescents with Internet Addiction Disorder: A tract-based spatial statistics study. *PLOS ONE,* 7(1), e30253. doi: 10.1371/journal.pone.0030253

Mayer, C. & Olds, T.S. (2012). Screen Time is More Strongly Associated than Physical Activity with Overweight and Obesity in 9- to 16-Year-Old Australians. *Acta Paediatrica*, 101(11) (November), pp. 1170–1174. doi: 10.1111/j.1651-2227.2012.02804.x. Epub 2012 Aug 23.

National Academy of Sports Medicine (author) & Sutton, B. G. (ed.) (2013). *NASM Essentials of Personal Fitness Training*, 4th edition. Baltimore, MD: Wolters Kluwer/Lippincott Williams & Wilkins.

Nauert, R. (2013). Significant Increase in ADHD Over Last 9 Years. *Psych Central*. Retrieved from http://psychcentral.com/news/2013/01/22/significant-increase-in-adhd-over-last-9-years/50668.html

PE4Life & Reed, K. (2012). *Game Changer: Phil Lawler's Crusade to Help Children by Improving Physical Education*. Champaign, IL: Human Kinetics.

Pellegrini, A. D., & Bjorklund, D. F. (1997). The Role of Recess in Children's Cognitive Performance. *Educational Psychologist*, 32(1), p. 35.

Platt, G. (2011). *Beating Dyspraxia with a Hop, Skip, and a Jump*. London: Jessica Kingsley Publishers.

Pytel, B. (2009). Pros and Cons of Recess Time in Schools: Is recess a mere tradition or a vital piece in education. *Suite101*. Retrieved from suite101.com

Raine, L. B., Lee, H. K., Saliba, B. J., Chaddock-Heyman, L., Hillman, C. H., & Kramer, A. F. (2013). The Influence of Childhood Aerobic Fitness on Learning and Memory. *PLOS ONE*, 8(9), e72666. doi: 10.1371/journal.pone.0072666

Rauner, R. R., Walters, R. W., Avery, M., & Wanser, T. J. (2013). Evidence that Aerobic Fitness is More Salient Than Weight Status in Predicting Standardized Math and Reading Outcomes in Fourth- Through Eighth-Grade Students. *Journal of Pediatrics*, 163(2) (August), pp. 344–348. doi: 10.1016/j.jpeds.2013.01.006

Reznik, M., Ozuah, P., et al. (2015). Incorporating Exercise into Classroom Lessons Increases Children's Physical Activity Levels. *Childhood Obesity*. Retrieved from http://www.sciencedaily.com/releases/2015/03/150325131407.htm

Ripley, A. (2013). *The Smartest Kids in the World: And how they got that way*. New York, NY: Simon and Schuster.

Slavin, R. (1991). *Student Team Learning: A practical guide to cooperative learning*, 3rd edition. Washington, DC: National Education Association.

Stoodley, C. J., & Fawcett, A. J. (2005). Impaired balancing ability in dyslexic children. *Experimental Brain Research*, 167(3) (December), pp. 370–380.

Twenge, J. (2010). Birth Cohort Increases in Psychopathology Among Young Americans, 1938–2007: A cross-temporal meta-analysis of the MMPI. *Clinical Psychology Review*, 30(2) (March), pp. 145–154.

Twenge, J. (2015). *Generation Me—Revised and Updated: Why Today's Young Americans Are More Confident, Assertive, Entitled—and More Miserable Than Ever Before.* New York, NY: Atria Books.

Zhou, Y., Fu-Chun Lin, F. C., Du, Y. S., Qin, L., et al. (2011). Gray Matter Abnormalities in Internet Addiction: A voxel-based morphometry study. *European Journal of Radiology*, 79(1) (July), pp. 92–95. doi: 10.1016/j.ejrad.2009.10.025

Online Sources

http://campustechnology.com/articles/2014/05/14/55-more-stem-students-fail-lectures-than-courses-with-active-learning.aspx?admgarea=News

http://www.dakmed.org/wp-content/uploads/2014/10/Integrating-Physical-Activity-throughout-the-School-Day.pdf

http://www.deadiversion.usdoj.gov/nflis/spec_rpt_adhd_2012.pdf

http://educationbythenumbers.org/content/high-school-test-scores-havent-improved-for-40-years-top-students-stagnating_251/

http://www.educationworld.com/a_curr/profdev/profdev174.shtml#sthash.Ghfoa5XK.dpuf

http://www.edutopia.org/blog/technology-teach-health-wellness-mary-beth-hertz

http://www.fastcoexist.com/3036607/this-school-has-bikes-instead-of-desks-and-it-turns-out-thats-a-better-way-to-learn

http://www.theguardian.com/society/2011/may/21/children-weaker-computers-replace-activity

http://www.humankinetics.com/excerpts/excerpts/classroom-behaviors

http://theinspiredtreehouse.com/child-development-core-strengthening-for-kids/

http://integratedlistening.com/case-studies/dyslexia-adhd-apd/

http://www.masslive.com/living/index.ssf/2013/09/more_americans_
exercise_at_work_with_desk_cycles_exercise_balls_as_chairs_treadmill_
desks.html

http://www.middleweb.com/5003/real-world-stem-problems/

http://www.murdochmethod.com/the-core-of-the-matter/

http://www.nytimes.com/1998/04/07/us/many-schools-putting-an-end-to-
child-s-play.html

http://www.ot-mom-learning-activities.com/core-exercises-for-kids.html

http://www.politico.com/story/2014/05/finland-school-system-107137

http://www.shapeamerica.org/advocacy/positionstatements/pe/loader.
cfm?csModule=security/getfile&pageid=4679

http://www.skillsforaction.com/DCD-and-dyspraxia

http://www.sparkpe.org/blog/how-physical-activity-affects-academic-
performance/

http://www.stemreports.com/wp-content/uploads/2011/06/NRC_STEM_2.
pdf

http://sydney.edu.au/compass/programs/teachers/resources/Core_
strength_-_HANDOUT.pdf

http://www.teachhub.com/top-12-classroom-fitness-activities

http://usatoday30.usatoday.com/news/education/2010-01-12-students-
depression-anxiety_N.htm

http://vestibular.org/understanding-vestibular-disorder/human-balance-system

http://www.webmd.com/add-adhd/guide/executive-function